Alaska's Sky Follies

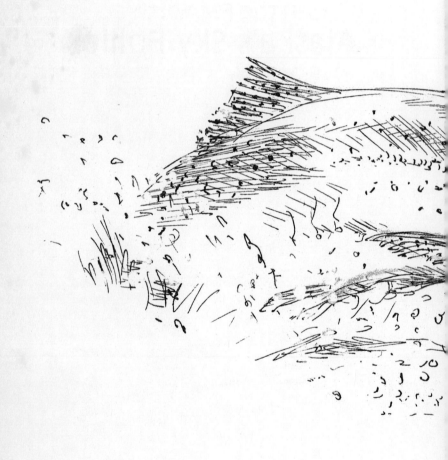

Alaska's Sky Follies
The Funny Side of Flying in the Far North

Joe Rychetnik

Epicenter Press
Fairbanks / Seattle

Editor: Don Graydon
Cover design: Elizabeth Watson
Cover and text illustrations: Sandy Jamieson
Inside design: Sue Mattson
Photos: Joe Rychetnik
Printer: Best Book Manufacturing

Library of Congress Cataloging-in-Publication Data

Rychetnik, Joe.
    Alaska's sky follies : the funny side of flying in the far
north / Joe Rychetnik.
        p. cm.
    ISBN 0-945397-44-5
    1. Bush flying—Alaska—Humor. 2. Rychetnik, Joe—
Anecdotes. I. Title.
TL522.A4R95   1995
629. 13'09798-dc20   95-31122
                                                          CIP

To order single, autographed copies of ALASKA'S SKY FOLLIES,
mail $13.95 each (Washington residents add $1.14 sales tax) plus
$2 for book rate shipping to: Epicenter Press, Box 82368, Kenmore,
WA 98028.

Booksellers: Retail discounts are available from our trade
distributor, Graphic Arts Center Publishing Co., Box 10306,
Portland, OR 97210. Phone 800-452-3032.

First Printing, September, 1995
10 9 8

PRINTED IN CANADA

For Howard Bowman, a master of the Alaskan sky and dear friend. May all your landings be happy ones.

And for the late Don Sheldon, one of Alaska's greatest bush pilots. May you rest forever on the home leg of an easy flight.

Don Sheldon at his Talkeetna airstrip in 1969.

Joe Rychetnik photo

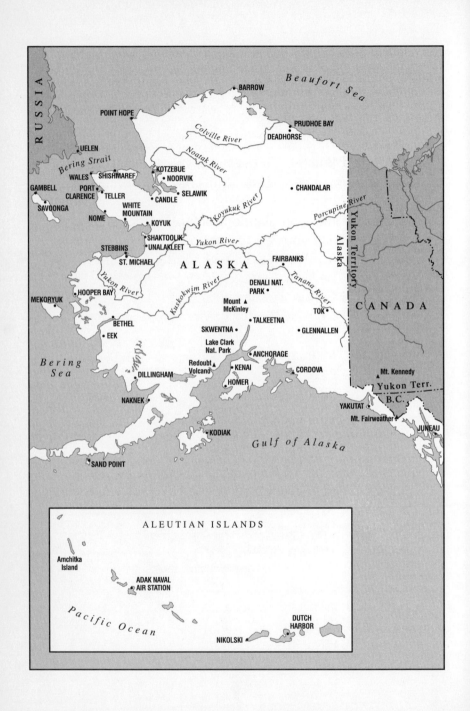

Table of Contents _____

Preface

Many people approach flying with a great deal of trepidation and are reluctant to assign their lives to someone who claims to know how to move them from A to B via the air currents. They count the number of engines and pilots, even cabin attendants, to give them confidence for boarding—the higher the number, the safer the plane. Even someone as experienced as my old friend Ray Smith, a senior captain for Delta Airlines, was seldom comfortable as a passenger in a single-engine job like a Cessna 180 or Piper Super Cub. After a flight around the McKinley peaks with Don Sheldon, the legendary Alaskan bush pilot, Ray was not ashamed to say he was "white-knuckle" all the way. He always felt that if he died in an air-related accident, it would be in such a crate.

But to see Alaska properly one must take to the air via the single-engine bush planes of the Cessna or Piper breed or something similar. They fly low and slow enough to let you visually enjoy the Great Land. These hops in small planes also make for the best stories because seemingly ordinary flights can turn into the wildest comedies. Without the Super Cub and her like, I wouldn't have much of a book. Some of the stories I tell here happened to me; others I heard about. Some of them even involve the Cub's big brothers, the multiengine planes that do a lot of Alaska's hauling.

Bush pilots, by the very nature of their business, have the potential for doing strange and funny things. I have a great respect for aviation and for the men and women who make their living flying in the Far North. They don't want to be the butt of humorous tales; they want to be allowed to die in peace at a ripe old age like the rest of us. But sometimes Lady Luck flings them a curve, and they become unwitting performers in an aerial circus. What you'll be reading about here are the top acts in these sky follies.

I got in on the fun simply because I was lucky enough to be in Alaska during a rich era for flying adventure. I showed up in Anchorage just after Alaska became a state, in 1959. Over the next dozen years, I logged thousands of miles as a bush-plane passenger in my work as a reporter and then a state trooper and then a Time-Life photographer. The blue yonder turned out to be even wilder than I thought.

These recollections aren't meant to embarrass or criticize any of Alaska's great bush pilots, who were doing what they thought was best at the time. But hindsight is always 20-20, and I have a great deal of that these days as I look back on my glorious times with some of the most fantastic characters Alaska has ever had to offer. You'll see that a lot of these adventures could have turned into disaster, but it's just human nature that near-tragedies become comedies in retrospect.

I've been warned by some dour folks that I shouldn't celebrate these high jinks because people are already too apprehensive about flying. But bush flights should be fun, and it's not my fault that many of them turned out to be funny as well. ✈

Acknowledgments _____

Dozens of Alaska's old-timers contributed to this collection of flying tales. They know who they are, and I thank them gratefully for their kindness in sharing their recollections with me. In particular I want to thank Bob Stevens, a retired Delta Airlines senior captain, whose two-volume *Alaskan Aviation History* was an inspiration; old Nome flying buddy Howard Bowman, now taking it easy on Lake Clark; and the man who continues to defy gravity in the Don Sheldon mode, Lowell Thomas, Jr.

I could not have gotten this act together without the constant prodding of my editor, Lael Morgan, and the support of the woman who would never fly in an airplane without four "motors" until she took to bush flying with a passion, my wife Glenda. ✈

Chapter 1

Madman Munz _____

Bill Munz put on a show for the folks of Nome one afternoon when he found the winds coming over the Nome Airport at exactly the same speed as his flying speed approaching the field. He came over the taxiway, cut back the engine, and the old Stinson Gull Wing just hung about fifteen feet in the air, the prop slowly turning. He set the controls and stepped down from the cabin to the rubber tire to accept a bottle of pop from a fellow in a pickup truck who was keeping the same slow pace as the airplane. In a few minutes half of Nome was at the field watching Munz ham it up.

But Bill Munz, who was reported to have had seven wives, was not the fun fellow he sometimes appeared to be. He was taciturn, sarcastic, anti-government to the point of jeopardizing people's safety, and far from a pleasant person to be with. I know, because I often had to use him as my pilot on my patrols as a state policeman. Munz constantly drummed his fingers on the instrument panel— "to keep the gauges free," he was wont to say. His radios, built by Marconi and glued into the fleet of Stinson Gull Wings he operated out of Nome, never worked or never worked when needed.

In 1960 I started to go on almost daily flying patrols

out of Nome, Unalakleet, Bethel, and Kotzebue, chauffeured by bush pilots in their light planes. My patrol limit stretched all the way along the Alaska coastline from the far northeast along the Beaufort Sea down the Chukchi and Bering sea coasts to Kuskokwim Bay.

My wife claimed I was gone from home five weeks out of the month, and in the air most of that time, and never in touch with her. She was about right, but it was a heady period of statehood, the early '60s. The state police force, with only sixty-six men, was stretched thin.

There were some fine bush pilots in those days, some as good as the pre-World War II old-timers. But unfortunately the state of Alaska made state policemen accept the lowest bid on bush flying. Therefore, my time in the air out of Nome was often spent with Bill Munz of Munz Northern Airways, the bargain-basement bush line. His unfortunate habits of not flying his flight plan and not landing at government-improved fields if he could help it and his irregular operating procedures—like not telling anyone where he was going—made my flying days a bit hairy.

The only other pilot of Munz Northern Airways was Ray Decker, a gentleman of the old school but scared to death of Munz and the possibility of losing his job. Ray was difficult to convince about things if they didn't conform to the Munz way of operation.

Once, flying back from Cape Espenberg and Shishmaref, I asked Ray if he didn't want to take on some fuel at Teller, where the trading post kept a few cases of Chevron for emergencies. He said he had enough and went on flying for Nome. When we got there, he pulled his usual stunt of flying down the Nome beach and buzzing his mobile home before landing at "Munz Field" at the end of the old Municipal Field. Munz and Decker refused to patronize Nome's FAA-approved airport.

We came in for a very steep landing and stopped at the far end of the field, where the Munz mechanic met us with a pickup truck. I didn't have a chance to ask Ray why we had stopped there instead of at the Munz hangar because he immediately jumped into the back of the pickup to avoid conversation. We dropped Ray off at the hangar, and I paid the mechanic five dollars to drive me home. On the way in, we talked about the weather and other things, and finally I asked him why Ray stopped the plane out at the far end of the airport.

"Out of gas, my guess!" he said. Ray told me later that Munz didn't like it when he bought gas out of town.

MUNZ WAS AN EXCELLENT PILOT who managed to keep his business profitable although he used ancient planes and had just one other pilot to assist him. But Munz drove me to distraction with his hatred of the Federal Aviation Administration, which maintained a foot-high file of violations on him but wouldn't go that final step of taking him to court or jerking his certificate, probably because of his violent temper and possible political connections. The officials with the FAA at Nome wouldn't touch him. They just wrote up each violation and added it to the board that hung in their office for all to see.

I much preferred to fly with Decker rather than Munz. My patrol flights were often long, and it was uncomfortable sitting next to a person I considered a madman. Munz's spiteful style came through loud and clear the day he had arranged to pick up his wife at 3 P.M. on the road to Solomon, where she was picking blueberries. She was just a minute late arriving at the spot where he was supposed to land his plane. She was still trudging up the hill, carrying two five-gallon buckets full of berries. So Munz just kept on flying to Nome.

I happened to be driving by, coming in from a patrol to Solomon. I offered her a ride, and she accepted. Bribery was far from my mind, but she did pour me a hat-full of ripe berries when I dropped her off at the Munz home, which consisted of a mobile home set up inside an old warehouse. I didn't think anything more about the incident until the next day, when Munz stormed into the state police office and told my wife to tell me to mind my own business when it came to his wife. He said he had wanted her to walk the fifteen miles into town to teach her a lesson in being prompt.

There was no way to get out of flying with Munz Northern unless the outfit was already booked up, because Bill Munz knew he was low bidder on any flight and would call Juneau and complain if I used another carrier. I kept telling my superiors that his airline wasn't safe, but they said the budget was the bottom line. I knew that eventually we would crash and I would have a case, but it took a while to happen. When it did, it was out on the Bering Sea ice, and Ray Decker was the pilot. Ray and I were stranded for four days, living on my emergency rations because the airplane carried none.

MY FAVORITE COMEDY SCENE involves the sulky and taciturn Bill Munz flying two Catholic nuns from Unalakleet to Nome one afternoon after sitting in the Unalakleet Lodge eating pie and coffee while the nuns made their gracious and time-consuming departure. He put the ladies on the back bench so they wouldn't disturb his reveries in the front of the plane.

He took off on skis and headed into the meek sunset. It was easy flying, with good visibility. Munz was wont to cut a corner here and there to save some gas, so he took a straight shot to Moses Point over the ice rather than follow the shore to Cape Denbeigh and hop across Norton Bay. Well over Norton Sound he discovered an almost uncontrollable urge to urinate. Up ahead was the large emergency field at Moses Point, which was kept ready for any kind of irregular traffic, cleared and well-lighted and open for business by FAA types.

Because of Munz's hatred of any form of government intrusion into the free skies and free land of the bush pilot, he refused to land there, instead telling the nuns he had to land on the shore ice to relieve himself.

He was within binocular vision of the people in the station office at the landing field, who wondered why the Gull Wing would risk landing on iffy shore ice when the airfield had acres of flat snow ready to accept the plane. They watched as Munz made a perfect landing on a chunk of ice, shut the engine down to a slow idle, emerged from the left-hand cabin door and walked behind the plane to the edge of the ice, and began to pee. Then it happened. The ice broke and dropped him into the water.

The nuns were belted in and probably didn't see his fall. But they certainly heard the curses as Munz thrashed around in his winter clothing, trying to gain a handhold and pull himself up from the water and back onto the ice. The boys at Moses Point were nearly dying with laughter as they watched the show through their binoculars. Munz finally got up on the ice, the water freezing on his jacket and pants, and clambered back into the cabin, shivering uncontrollably. He got the engine roaring and turned up the cabin heat as he tried to find a safe path across the ice sheet to gain flying speed.

One of the nuns told me she prayed. The other nun said she couldn't stop smiling as he yelled at them to shut up when they sympathized with him, saying, "You poor man!" ✈

Chapter 2

Flying Fool _____

My worst nightmare with Bill Munz himself as pilot came true the day he flew me to the Coast Guard's Loran station at Port Clarence on the Bering Sea. The commanding officer had requested a civilian investigator to check on missing building materials. The Loran tower was the magic navigational facility that kept U.S. submarines on course. Its tower was taller than the Empire State Building—1,350 feet, if I remember correctly—and it was held erect by perfect balance and dozens of thick steel cables anchored to the ground by concrete deadmen.

The station had a crew of about fifteen. It was a one-year voluntary assignment—not often repeated, they say, as this place was off by itself and had the look of a maximum security prison from the outside. In hostile weather in this exposed coastal location, it was just that for the men inside.

The station was losing building materials from its stockpile during the long hours of darkness, even when precautions were taken to secure the area. There was no exterior guard, but lights were spotted over the piles of lumber, wire, and other materials. The raider, using a dog sled because it made less noise than a snowmachine, simply knocked out the lightbulb or waited until it burned out. Then he would load up and be gone. It was a relatively easy place to make off with free building supplies, and several thousands of dollars worth had been taken. It wouldn't be hard to get up to this figure, because something as basic as a six-foot-long two-by-four had a twenty-dollar price tag on it up there.

I asked Ray Decker to fly me there on short notice because I had court the next day. We also had to hurry to beat a low-pressure system moving in from Siberia. Ray couldn't do it, but he said Munz would run me up the coast after lunch. The weather was perfect, and I was looking forward to getting to the station and seeing this monster of a landmark at close range.

The station had a two-mile-long runway for the C-130 supply planes that came in from time to time. Half the runway was kept cleared of snow. The other half was kept in graded snow for ski planes. I told Munz that the station commander had recommended we land on the cleared area, which they had just plowed down to the gravel for our arrival. The parking apron was concrete, so we would never even get our shoes wet. I was in full uniform, too.

AS WE APPROACHED the tall beacon, I noticed that Munz was not making an approach for the landing field, which stretched out to the north. Instead, it looked like he was planning to land in among the giant cables that held up the tower and then taxi up to a bunker door on the offside of the building. I reminded him that the runway was cleared for him.

Munz gave me the finger, a sign I got used to him using whenever the hated subject of Uncle Sam came up.

"Bill, land on the strip!" I yelled.

All he said was "Fuck 'em!" and down we came like a

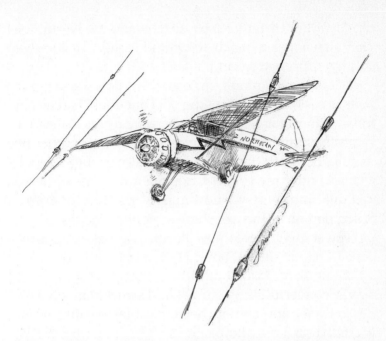

fighter plane avoiding a chasing Focke Wolf 190, weaving through the pattern of giant cables that held up the tower. Any one of these cables could have sliced off a wing. I could see us plunging to our deaths as the tower collapsed! But Bill kept flying in, and after getting near the bunker door, set the Gull Wing down on the snow and skidded up to the structure.

I got out, glad to be alive and wondering how in the world we would get the plane out of that spider's web of death. But suddenly I had my hands full with a red-faced C.O. and three other Coasties screaming at me. I was pushed inside the building and surrounded by hostile men, all yelling at once.

"What in hell do you mean flying through our cable farm and landing off the strip, you dumb sonofabitch!" I was shown a huge window that overlooked a perfectly clear landing strip that seemed to run to the North Pole. They all pointed in that direction and yelled, "That's where you are supposed to land, idiot!"

It took a few minutes to cool them down and get the point across that I was not the pilot and that I had no control over the pilot, who was chartered to fly me to the Coast Guard base and had done it his way. It was another five minutes before the skipper calmed down enough to apologize and offer me coffee. I explained the type of person that Bill Munz was and how mere suggestion, or even an order, had no influence whatsoever on his plans.

The skipper's eyes now lit up. "I guess we got us a Gull-Winged Stinson, boys! He's not going to be able to fly out of there. I won't allow him to try." I told him that was a wonderful decision, as I had sweated blood as we missed one- and two-inch-thick cables coming in and wanted a safer way home.

"Tell that dumb bastard that he can either taxi the plane around the station and onto the cleared tie-down apron or plan to leave it here, as I forbid him to fly out, and you'd better do it now while we have daylight."

I went out to see Munz. He was sitting in the cockpit, drumming his fingers on the instrument panel. I told him what the Coast Guard skipper had told me, and I asked him to taxi the plane around to the airstrip. Munz ordered me into the plane. I figured he needed my eyes on that side of the cockpit while we taxied around the station. Instead, he revved up the Wright engine and found a few feet to run and took off into the pattern of cables. We were airborne and dodging cables before I knew it.

"OK, Bill, we know you are a great pilot," I told him. "Now will you land on the strip so I can finish my business!" I was getting as mad as I was scared.

He gave me the finger and said "Fuck 'em" and flew us back to Nome.

He had his girl deliver a bill the next day for the flight. He wrote on the bill in longhand, "You were taken to Port Clarence Coast Guard and brought home—pay up or I'll take it to Juneau!"   ✈

Chapter 3

Elastic Scarelines _____

The airline that served Nome was known far and wide as "Elastic Scarelines" for a variety of reasons, all having to do with poor service and planes that sometimes didn't fly. No relation to the slick Alaska Airlines of later years, which became a national leader in customer satisfaction and always got my nod when I headed north. Back then, Elastic was too big an outfit to be considered a bush airline, but its operations had all the elements of Keystone Cops comedy, and a book could be written about this hee-haw of air carriers.

I was in Nome as a member of the Alaska State Police to pick up an unhappy prisoner and take him via Elastic to the state jail in Anchorage. At that time, the early '60s, Alaska had no prison system, and a sentence of less than one year would be served in one of the larger state jails. For sentences that carried more than a year of penal servitude, prisoners were taken to a federal penitentiary in the South 48.

Alaska was billed about ninety-five dollars a day for such upkeep—so sentences were always short. No such prison sentences as life or ninety-nine years, because the few Alaskans back home were reluctant to see their tax money spent to support a miscreant who would be living a step or two above his usual standard in the Big House. Of course, oil money has now given Alaska its own prison system, and the two- and three-year murder sentences once meted out have become historical oddities.

My traveling companion had hurled a 350-pound anvil through his brother, killing him dead on the first try. But in those early days of statehood, DAs and judges often downgraded high crime to fit the budget—things very close to murder often were listed as disorderly conduct.

Elastic Scarelines had a hard time staffing its stewardess department and had been recruiting English-speaking German girls of great beauty and charm who happened to know absolutely nothing about life, in or out of Alaska. On this flight, the Lorelei came over to where we were sitting, the hulking prisoner handcuffed to a belly chain. The only airlines in these United States that allowed such travel of prisoners were those in Alaska. The stewardess asked me for my service revolver.

I told her the revolver was part of my uniform and that I could not give it to her. The rule in the state police was to never carry a loaded revolver in a plane but to make everyone believe it was loaded. I didn't want my traveling partner to think anything else. The stewardess smiled and moved on down the aisle, assisting other passengers, her great looks giving all the bush people a thrill.

Moments later she was back, stating that I must give her my gun because the captain demanded it. I again refused and told her to bring the pilot to me if there was any question.

Ten minutes later she was back again. If I wouldn't give her the gun, I must give her the bullets! I again refused. I thought I was home free. In ninety minutes we would be in Anchorage, and I could lodge the big man in the state jail and have a nice dinner without him.

By this time the meals were being passed out. I told the woman delivering the meals that for safety's sake, we wanted no food or drink. But then her colleague suddenly returned to tell me she could not feed us unless I gave her at least one bullet. About then it became pretty clear that the pilots were pulling a gag on her. I told her that I wanted no food served to us but that I'd be pleased to give her one bullet if she would leave us be until we arrived in Anchorage. She took the cartridge I slipped from my gun belt, wrapped it in a napkin, and headed for the cockpit.

The next thing I knew, she put two trays of food in front of us. I told her to please remove the trays and skip us. She jerked back the trays and said in a voice that was meant to be heard throughout the cabin that I was being cruel to my prisoner. She had seen my kind in Germany during the war, she said. So now I was being compared with a storm trooper or the Gestapo.

Five minutes later she returned and demanded that I remove at least one handcuff from the prisoner to let him eat. Passengers around me began muttering that I was cruel and that they had never seen anything like this.

I told her I would remove one cuff but couldn't hold myself responsible. As soon as the tray was delivered to my anvil-heaver, he used his free hand to fling it as far as he could, covering several rows of passengers with string beans, hamburger steak, mashed potatoes, and coffee. In the bedlam, I quickly snared the free hand and recuffed it to the belly chain. My uniform was a mess, but in worse shape were the folks trying to clean the food from their hair.

Both stewardesses were raking me over the coals now, and my murderous partner was laughing. Luckily we were approaching Anchorage, and I prayed nothing else would happen. We were first off the DC-6, and I practically dragged my prisoner from the plane. I was just about settled into the waiting police car when it was halted by the blonde goddess from Marburg, rapping on the window.

"You forgot your bullet!" she yelled at me.

"It's quite all right—we have more," I told her.

"But I insist you take it. This is my first flight and I don't want any bad marks on my record." She handed me the cartridge wrapped in a paper napkin.

IN FAIRBANKS ONE WINTER'S DAY, I arrived at the airport with half a dozen prisoners to move to Anchorage and points south. These were all full fares for Elastic Scarelines and its new jets—which the company was anxious to fill any way it could.

After an hour's wait, I began thinking about switching to a Pan Am jet due to arrive right away. But I knew the state legislators preferred we spend our state police money with firms that had the word Alaska in their names. I was assured the Alaska jet would be in shortly. I watched as the Pan Am jet landed and then left without a full load.

After another hour, I left the airport security office, where my charges were safely handcuffed to a steam pipe, and visited a friend who was working at Flight Service in the FAA tower.

"Hi, Jim, any word on that Alaska jet's arrival?" I asked him. "We have a half-dozen convicts we will have to feed pretty soon if we don't get them on board."

"What Alaska jet is that, Joe?" he asked.

"The one that was supposed to have left two and a half hours ago to Anchorage and Seattle," I told him.

Our airplane, he told me, was just that minute leaving Frankfurt, West Germany, with a load of NATO troops. The airlines didn't have anything skedded in to Fairbanks until the next morning.

"You mean we're stuck here overnight?" I asked in disbelief. "We could have switched to Pan Am if they had told us!"

And sure enough, I got back to the security office just in time to hear the flight cancellation notice delivered on the PA system. The ticket agents never even blushed when I questioned them. Business was business!

I CAN'T LET MY Elastic Scarelines tales end without the story of a hairy winter day in Kotzebue. I was standing at the terminal with Joe Brantley, the one-man Kotzebue police force, hoping to catch a ride to Fairbanks when we heard the four-engine plane approaching the field. The fog was thick and drifting in wool-like waves across the taxiway, and the plane's first pass was high over the field.

Waiting passengers, mostly Eskimos going to the big city and state employees like myself, were hoping the weather would break long enough to allow a safe landing. After that, the plane shouldn't have any problem taking off in limited visibility because there were no hills or mountains nearby.

The plane roared overhead six more times. Joe suggested we go up in the tower and listen to the crew there talk down the big transport. With a full load of passengers, almost all with Kotzebue as their final destination, the captain would make every effort to get the plane down. Fairbanks was 500 miles away and Nome was 120 miles to the south, so landing in Kotzebue would be the answer to everyone's problem.

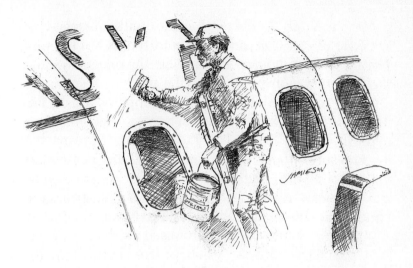

Lower and lower the plane came, the flight service operators telling the pilot they saw breaks in the fog on the runway and suggesting he come lower to take advantage of them. Of course, it was the captain's decision, and the fellows who flew the Alaska routes for any of the major airlines had plenty of experience with Alaska weather.

The plane came lower still, and Joe thought he saw the wing go by. The plane swung out over Kotzebue Sound another time, taking the transport even lower. We counted a dozen passes now, and I was wondering when the captain would just give up. But he radioed that he could see bits and patches of the runway, and because the peninsula Kotzebue is on has no hills or tall structures, the low passes were safe.

This time the plane was really low. The pilot reported he could see the ground as he made his final final approach with the obvious intent to land. We saw the big plane skim by and set down in the drifting fog. But it looked to us like it landed on its belly. It seemed to slide on the icy surface forever—or at least until it reached the snow berms pushed up by plows at the end of the runway. The silver monster slid up onto the piled snow and stopped. It was then we heard the copilot's response to the landing: "Oh, shit!" After all the approaches, on this one he forgot to lower the landing gear.

Several vehicles raced over to the stranded plane, but there was no fire or other emergency. The passengers stepped right from the cabin door onto the packed snow and onto the taxiway. Joe suggested I stay overnight at his place as this looked like the end to Elastic Scarelines' efforts to levitate me to the promised Fairbanks. As we left the scene, a fellow, no doubt ordered in by corporate headquarters, was seen out on the wing with a paint can and brush, blacking out the airline's logo.

The hulk rested there for several weeks until it was towed to the junk pile nearby. An enterprising Kotzebue businessman applied to the village council for permission to open up a night club in the perfectly suitable fuselage. Names were suggested like "Silver Bullet Lounge" and "The 13th Pass." But the village was a dry community— no booze allowed—and the council wouldn't allow a night club on the edge of town under any name. ✈

Chapter 4

Fish Tale _____

After statehood in 1959, the major airlines had bush operations in hub cities and villages like Nome, Kotzebue, Bethel, Unalakleet, Dillingham, Homer, and Kodiak. Many bush organizations operated out of Fairbanks and Anchorage. One of the great pioneer airlines of Alaska, Wien, had a very fine bush operation in Nome and Fairbanks. Most of the smaller bush operators flew under what is known as an air taxi certificate, which offered a great deal of flexibility.

Some of the air cargo companies that operated surplus multiengine military aircraft were run much like bush airlines, taking work where they could find it and flying into and out of all sorts of squeaky places.

I recall needing an immediate flight to Unalakleet from Anchorage to pick up an important piece of police evidence. The FAA advised me that the next flight to that Eskimo village on the eastern end of Norton Sound was a cargo flight, using a C-46 Curtiss Commando. The Commando had survived World War II to fly freight in the Far North.

I signed a waiver with the captain, a young fellow who looked a lot like Smilin' Jack of comic-strip fame. He said his plane was not certificated to fly passengers, but if I helped load and didn't mind a bucket seat, I would be welcome. The cargo would be salmon, once we got to Unalakleet. He didn't say fresh-caught or that dozens of plastic tubs of the Native harvest from Norton Sound and the Bering Sea would fill the belly of the big twin-engine Commando.

IT WAS A JOLLY FLIGHT over to Unalakleet as he kept the plane low and tended to harass moose along the way. It was still daylight when we landed, and the loading process began without fanfare. I received my package of evidence and was immediately pressed into helping load the open-topped plastic tubs filled with pink and chum salmon. The tubs came complete with a coating of flies and other insects looking for a free ride.

A flatbed truck loaded with the tubs backed up to the gaping cargo door, and two husky villagers heaved each tub into the doorway. We in the plane skidded the heavy tubs back toward the tail until the deck was solid salmon. The tubs filled the cargo deck, and still there were more. We piled the extra tubs atop the others, which were already less than secure because they had no place for attaching a rope to keep them in place. We also loaded a tub of crab for the crew to divide—if and when we got back to Anchorage.

The boss of the loaders told the pilot that all the salmon were caught as they were heading back to their native waters and this would help guide the plane east to Anchorage!

The pilot and copilot occupied their seats and the engineer sat in his jump seat. I made do by sitting on an empty Chevron case that was bungee-corded to the bulkhead behind the cockpit area. I had no seat belt.

The noisy, heavy plane trundled its way to the end of the gravel runway, turned around with a roar, and made the usual run-up. It was painfully obvious that earplugs would have helped. Then the silver whale slowly started its roll down the bumpy strip, and the pilot pulled the control column back to take us airborne—and at that moment the plastic tubs of fish, lubricated with slime and water, began bouncing and sliding and dumping to the rear of the plane.

The Commando was now in the air, and the pilot said he thought he would be able to keep it that way. But he said it would be a more stable vehicle if the copilot, engineer, and I would get in the back and "square things away" for level flight.

With chums and pinks slithering here and there, and no way to set up orderly lines of tubs again, we had to settle for an even spreading of salmon over the whole area and hope that the plane wouldn't maneuver too much and destabilize the load. Everything went OK the rest of the way, although we were all covered in fish slime and abuzz with flies.

SMILIN' JACK KNEW that with the slippin' and slidin' load of fish, he couldn't make a steep descent into Anchorage. He advised the tower that he would be dropping down in elevation well out of town and would make a very low approach to the runway. So far so good. We crossed our fingers that the landing would be gentle.

The landing was as perfect as you could find on Air France or Pan Am. The salmon knew they had one last hump to make on their way to their home spawning waters, so most of them slid toward the cargo door area. There was little we could do to prevent this. The law of gravity prevailed.

The ground crew was anxious to get the fish unloaded and trucked to the cannery. No amount of shouting from the cockpit window, trying to warn them about all the fish on the loose, would halt the impetuous ground crew. As soon as the props stopped, the crew had the truck backed up to the plane and the door latch lifted. The avalanche of not-so-fresh fish was totally unexpected. The unloaders got battered by descending chums and pinks, while we did our best to keep from laughing in their surprised faces.

I grabbed my evidence package and slid down with the fish, almost as stinky as the salmon.

"Hey, Joe, you forgot your crab," the crew chief shouted after me. But I wanted nothing more to do with the harvest of the sea. My kids hosed me off when I got home. ✈

Chapter 5

The Story
Behind the Story _____

No book on Alaska's bush pilots could evolve without a chapter devoted to Don Sheldon, of Talkeetna. A million words have been written about this famous pilot and his exploits. He was good copy for both the journalist and the feature writer as his very appearance and personality were noteworthy. Couple that with his mighty deeds, and you have a flier that for sheer production of rescues, records, and reconnaissance of Alaska's vertical geography towers above all the rest.

James Greiner's *Wager with the Wind: The Don Sheldon Story*, published in 1974 by Rand McNally, tells but a seventh of the story of this towering iceberg of a man, but tells it well. My son David Rychetnik produced a terrific thirty-minute special for public television that year, but with its pictorial approach it could tell even less of the Sheldon story, which goes on and on like a Norse saga. Perhaps the most candid of all reports—"Off into the Wild White Yonder," by Coles Phinizy for the February 14, 1972, issue of *Sports Illustrated*—comes closest to the man in the fewest number of words.

I was fortunate to have fellow *Sports Illustrated* writer Phinizy in tow in Alaska in 1971. I suggested he start his Don Sheldon research by spending some time at Evil Alice

Powell's Talkeetna Motel, where he could view Sheldon from a distance like some bird-watcher.

Coles wasn't about to be put on by some pumped-up "good ol' boy" who needed some free press. He wanted to "check this fellow out," and in so doing he fell head over heels in love with the character and did a superb job in his magazine story about Sheldon.

COLES WAS NOT a man without devious ways to expose the real person behind the image. One afternoon when things were slow at the Talkeetna Motel bar, he drifted in, hoping to snag the first drink of the day. It was about two. Alice usually left the bar wide open while she tended to making things like her Fiddlehead Sauce Alicia, local blueberry pie, and sourdough rolls. Then she would barricade herself against intrusion and nap for a good ninety minutes, until the sun really slipped over the yardarm. Then she would change into something from Neiman Marcus and become the grande dame hostess she loved to be.

Alice was a very well-educated lady from upstate New York and a near-Olympic skater with many years of Lake Placid training. She knew everyone in Alaska from the governor on down. Her nickname "Evil Alice" was never used to her face, although some of the kids who made money by picking fiddlehead ferns for her would sometimes try to get away with it. She was quick to bring them up short, informing them that she is "Mrs. Powell"— "Alice" to her friends.

The bar was officially open whenever Alice said it was. But to cater to thirsty locals, she allowed some self-service. She never lost a dime from villagers and guests helping themselves to the Bud or Oly and leaving a mark on the pad at the register. She was always able to take in a few shekels from the early drinkers she would otherwise miss. Talkeetna was mostly a bottled-beer burg and Oly was king; Miller and Bud trailed behind, with mixed drinks almost never ordered. Alice called herself "the Li'l Ol' Beertender."

On special days when she had a new frock or pantsuit to audition, she would take the Waring blender from the locked cabinet and make a mess of melt-in-your-mouth daiquiris, but this didn't happen often. Her husband, Sherm, didn't like to wash all those glasses.

This afternoon Coles made his way around the bar, found the ice machine, loaded up the bar supply tub, and proceeded to mix what he called "the Ultimate Martini." It was his umbilical cord to Rockefeller Center and the Time-Life publishing empire.

The creation of the Ultimate Martini all had to do with keeping a glacial chill on every utensil and vessel, including the serving glass. He would prefer that the bartender keep his fingers up to the second knuckle in the ice supply.

Running his eyes over the row of gin bottles, he was astounded to see nothing more prestigious than Gordon's. A bottle of Gordon's was duly buried in the ice, as was a set of Alice's best glasses: the big-bowled champagne bird-baths that she used to toast twenty-fifth anniversaries and the like. He tossed in the stainless steel swizzle spoon for good measure. There was a bottle of red-stuffed olives, and an ancient bottle of LeJon vermouth that rested on the edge of the ice tub. It was all in keeping with Alaska's icy past, Coles said.

While Coles was getting his martini factory in order, one of the Talkeetna old-timers wandered in looking for

Alice on some pretext, but hoping to add another Oly to his yard-long tab. He was mesmerized by Cole's preparations. This retired miner from the Peters Creek District had never seen, savored, or swilled a martini, and Coles was happy to have an unjaded guinea pig to test his formula on. While waiting for the chill to set in, Coles pumped the old-timer for stories about Don Sheldon, getting more material than he could jot down.

The miner told Coles about Sheldon dropping cases of dynamite from his plane to within twenty steps of the mine bunkhouse. He told Coles that it took real skill to lay those cases of Hercules right down by the door, instead of a day's walk into the tailings—or through the bunkhouse roof. Coles agreed it was real bush flying. Coles was not aware of the Alaskan technique used to deliver everything from Anacin to bathtubs when landing fields were spongy and the local rivers and lakes were ice-filled. Coles later referred to it as "skip bombing," a World War II term. In Alaska, it's called "uppa you ass."

COLES POURED THE OLD MINER the first glass of Ultimate Martini. Both men sipped the crystal-clear fluid with the look of scientists seeking the mythical fountain of youth.

"The trick is to get just a millimicron coating of vermouth over the body of icy gin. It takes a sprayer but I don't have one here," Coles confided to the old-timer, who was beginning to enjoy his scientific work. "The next one will be a tad less. Bottoms up." And Coles returned to improving on the drink.

By this time several members of the midafternoon crowd were watching the show. These are folks who would normally help themselves to an Oly or a Miller and

sit out front sucking on the bottle until Alice came along to collect. But now they were asking Coles if they could be included in the taste test. None of them had heard of a "martooney" except in the movies.

"The Thin Man used to drink 'em and feed 'em to his dog Asta," a film buff reported.

Coles upped the production, and he watched his vermouth application with greater care. Everyone agreed that it was an improved drink, although most did not know what he was talking about, Coles having a kind of flim-flam delivery. They just swallowed the whole glass-full after the first sip, taking his word for the nuances explained along the way.

"Gentlemen, the proper martini must be sipped!" Coles announced, and began mixing batch number three, again with clinical restraint on use of the shabby vermouth bottle.

"Any of you fellows know Don Sheldon, the pilot?" Coles asked his tasting class. In this log-cabin village of less than two hundred souls, nearly everyone had their roof shingles loosened by Sheldon's low approaches and overloaded takeoffs. "Yeah, we know Don—one helluva a pilot," they agreed.

THE AFTERNOON WORE ON, and when Alice got up from her nap, she found the bar full of happy people, a man named Coles Phinizy, from New York, serving the drinks, and six empty Gordon's gin bottles in the garbage.

Rather than stop the fun, she came over to where I was cleaning the afternoon's salmon catch and asked about this stranger behind the bar.

"Is his credit any good?"

"Alice, you're from Lake Placid yourself. I should think you could judge the cut of his jib better than I, a dumb bohunk from Chicago."

"I never heard of this *Sports Illustrated* outfit he claims to write for," she went on.

"Alice, he is one of the finest of the Time-Life sportswriters, with a salary in five figures, and he's here on an assignment with an expense account to cover his living."

"Well, he's got the bar full of deadbeats and they are all talking about Don Sheldon and they are drinking me dry of Gordon's gin and there is not one penny rung up on the cash register."

"I can tell you these big-time correspondents have lush expense accounts, Alice. It will all be covered when things calm down."

"Well then, it looks like it's my best afternoon since the first of the year. How does five hundred dollars sound, Joe?" she asked after she peeked into the overflowing bar, where the village was gathered for free booze. "Guess I better get over there and try out one of his martooneys. I hear they have olives in them."

I walked over to where the martini master was holding forth, having run through the Gordon's and now into Gilbey's as he collected more of the goods on Sheldon.

"You sure have a way with the townsfolk, Coles! What a way to sneak up on your quarry and surround him with a persona ready-built," I said with a smile.

"Hey, Joe, try one of these!" he said. "I think I got it right; I stopped using that LeJon and am going pure gin with a drop of juice from the olive jar."

"How much do you have down on the great flier of McKinley?" I asked.

"Not a goddam thing. I keep hearing one impossible story after another, so I know he's got this place in his pocket. I'm just waiting for ol' twinkle eyes himself to come in, and I'll lay my truth serum on him."

"I'm afraid you'll wait a long time, Coles," Alice said from the other end of the bar as she rescued her best glassware from destruction. "Don don't drink! That fellow lives on oatmeal with brown sugar and strong tea."

She went on: "Coles, have you ever considered joining the bartenders union? I have never seen such a happy crowd since New Year's Eve.

"I'd put you on at ten dollars an hour plus tips," she said with a wink. "Even throw in the dinner meal."

"Sorry, Alice. As a salaried employee of Time-Life, I am not allowed to mix pleasure with work. But if you would ever get in some decent makings, I may put on a return engagement," he said as he poured the last of the Gilbey's into his glass.

For those not privy to the high life enjoyed by the big-name writers of the big-name magazines, an arrangement was worked out whereby a flyspecked Talkeetna Air Ser-

vice letterhead was craftily altered to appear to be a bill-
ing for one afternoon of mountain flying by the mighty
Don Sheldon—price, five hundred dollars. It was a fair
deal for getting the log-cabin village off the ground for
one afternoon via martini jet-assist. Time-Life got a
bargain. ✈

Chapter 6

The Most Famous
Bush Pilot of All _____

Donald Edward Sheldon was born in the heart of the
Rocky Mountains and grew up in a region rich in the history and resources needed to keep an adventurous lad
interested in life. It was an ideal setting for developing
the character and skills required for Alaska.

Mount Morrison, Colorado, was his birthplace, but the
family moved shortly afterward to the South Park district
of the Rockies in Wyoming, where the mountain men of
the nineteenth century had wrested a living from the wilderness. Their trails from the early 1800s are still there, as
is the Oregon Trail that wound its way west not too far
from the Sheldon family farm.

In 1934, when the worldwide depression was bottom-
ing out and jobs of any kind were scarce, thirteen-year-
old Don took a backbreaking job with the Wyoming Tie
and Timber Company, an outfit that produced railroad
ties. The job brought him the adventure of the woods and
the excitement of big log floats down the Wind River. He
would never be content sitting behind a desk or wearing
a tie.

From the shadow of Wyoming's highest mountain,
Gannett Peak, Sheldon and two friends drove a Model A
Ford to a Seattle dock. The boat to Alaska had just left.

His companions found enough excitement in the bustling seaport of Seattle to last them until they decided to head south to the Oregon fruit farms, where jobs picking apples and pears were a sure way to get rich. Don waited for the next boat to Alaska. He fell in love with the Inside Passage on his way north to Seward and then came up with just enough cash to ride the train to Anchorage.

Working as a milk-bottle washer in the town's Step and a Half Dairy gave him a look into another industry he would avoid in the future. He headed north with all the cash he made after a few weeks in Anchorage and went on up to Talkeetna.

Depending on where you drink and who you ask, "Talkeetna" is supposed to mean "river of plenty." "Na" means "river" and is a well-established suffix all over the Athabaskan region. The area of this log-cabin village is certainly blessed with plenty: salmon, trout, moose, caribou, bears, berries, and gold in them thar hills. Adjacent to the Susitna, Chulitna, and Talkeetna rivers, few places are as well-situated as the village of Talkeetna. I lived there on and off for many years and loved every moment of it. Don found it to be paradise in 1938.

The trials and tragedies of his early years serving the transportation needs of this most beautiful part of Alaska are well-recorded elsewhere. My goal here is to mine some of the humor that accompanied him everywhere he went.

As a new staff photographer and feature reporter for the *Anchorage Daily Times,* I grew to know the road to Talkeetna by heart and flew with Don or his sidekick Mike Fisher often. I knew I was witnessing a piece of Alaskan history that would soon vanish.

ON A SUPPLY FLIGHT to the Peters Creek mining

district, I was in the rear tandem seat as Don Sheldon flew the Super Cub with the big tires. The caretaker who had snowshoed out to the diggings from Trappers Creek was low on food and radio batteries. The supply pack for him was on my lap: a well-bundled mix of groceries and Eveready Dry Cells.

The breakup of winter ice had left the mining camp in acres of mushy snow and muddy potholes. It was obvious there would be no landing. The miner waved as we circled overhead, and Don yelled back to me to be ready to shove the forty-pound case of groceries out of the plane when he gave the word. We didn't want to bury the box in a snowbank or, worse, drop it onto a roof of one of the outbuildings. Don would make a low-level swoop so the box would skid or roll to a stop where the miner could easily find it.

The first swoop was too high, so Don circled again and came in just inches above what would be terra firma if there was any firma at all. The big wheels plowed up a furrow of muddy snow and water as we skimmed by the waiting man, getting him wet enough to not mind the splash the box made when it bounced once and spun into a pothole, again dousing him.

We circled the scene to see that everything was OK as the recipient lugged the box to a shop table near some machinery. He sliced the lid off in one neat move and quickly pawed through the supplies. Don said later that when he saw the man pull just the broken neck of a Jack Daniels bottle out of the box, he knew we were both better off not being there. Later deliveries were along more standard lines, with the booze arriving uninjured.

Dropping supplies from the air was a specialty of Don's. He said his years flying in B-17s during World War

II taught him a lot. Dropping items like pills, medicine, and other things that would fit into the hollow of a roll of toilet paper got to be a game as Don would try to bounce the roll at the feet of the recipient. In case he overflew the target, the unwinding roll of toilet paper would mark the spot.

MANY YEARS LATER, up in the Brooks Range, I was location director for an NBC-TV special called "The Wolf Men." We were based at Red Adney's hunting lodge, and every morning I'd be out with Don in his Super Cub, searching for wolves or caribou for the camera crew.

Flying over No Name Lake, two valleys west from Lake Chandalar, Don noticed a man violently waving a flag of some sort. He insisted we investigate, as he loved to do good deeds on someone else's dollar. The Super Cub slid to a stop on the snow-covered lake but sank enough into what was incipient slush to make Don cautious about promising to deliver a kitchen sink or bathtub, he told me later.

A fur-clad man walked down from the cabin nestled above the shore and told us he was Professor So-and-So from the University of California. He was living for a year in that remote valley with his wife and two sons to re-search the problems of primitive survival with just basic tools. His problem was that he was plumb out of 16mm ECO color movie film for his Bolex. Could we pick up some film, pay for it with his traveler's checks, and drop it off soon—like today?

I took the order, but told him it could be as long as a week before we got back with the film. ECO is commer-cial Ektachrome sold only to pros, and I had never seen it in Anchorage or Fairbanks as it was always a special-order item from Rochester, New York. We agreed to do our best, and Don wrote down the trip as he would any other bush flight business.

On takeoff, the Super Cub leaped into the air right at the point where the slush ended and the brush began, a nice thing when one is five hundred miles from home and Band-Aids.

Don's assistant Mike Fisher flew me into Fairbanks in the 180 and I checked photo stores, with no luck. I finally called Anchorage, and Steve McCutcheon at Mac's Foto Service said he had twenty rolls in his home freezer—hundreds of dollars worth. I told Steve to put them in a stout box and send them to Fairbanks, in care of the Wien Alaska Airways ticket counter, along with his bill. Little did we know how lucky we were, because it turned out that Steve would not order ECO ever again.

When I got the film, I lined up the six-inch by six-inch cartons one atop the other and duct-taped them into a three-foot-long bomb. I created a duct tape loop at the top end, and from scrap toweling in Red Adney's storeroom made a red-and-white tail ten feet long. We loaded the film into the Super Cub, planning to deliver it when we could.

Day after day we sought the wily caribou on NBC-TV's nickel, the silver-and-red bomb of film resting behind the backseat of the Super Cub. One afternoon, returning to Chandalar without sighting any caribou, Don said he would give the valley of the primitives a buzz. Sure enough, there was the log cabin and the muddy shoreline tracks where the professor and his family trudged for water. Don said we would drop the film on the next pass. The professor emerged from the cabin and ran, waving, away from the cabin.

Don told me to drop the film when he yelled. I had the fabric tail in one hand and the long bomb in my lap, ready to heave it out.

"Try not to hit the fella," Don yelled back as we made the run to what all bombardiers know as the release point. Looking down, I could see the fur-clad man running around in wild circles instead of standing still. Don made a steep bank and yelled "Bombs away!" Down the bomb went, its tail whipping out the door. We zoomed up steeply, then banked again to watch.

Down went the bomb with ever-increasing speed. I had the feeling that the fellow down there with all the degrees and a Ph.D. behind his name was trying to catch this thing that weighed about twenty pounds and was moving in a blur. Like watching a great fielding play by Jose Canseco, the blur of the bomb merged with the furry man. Then there was a spout of muddy water that shot up twenty feet or more.

"Does he look OK?" Don yelled back.

I hollered that he might be wet and muddy, but by God he was waving at us.

I found out almost a year later that the film bomb had zipped right between our wilderness man's hands and drilled a hole in the muddy tundra at his feet. A couple of inches closer and it would have rammed his head into the earth. It was a close call, but like people keep saying, any landing you walk away from is a happy one. And I learned that if you're expecting something by air delivery, stay the hell out of the drop zone. The tail on the bomb is there to mark the landing spot, not your grave! ➤

Chapter 7

Missionary's Position ___

Before World War II, many Native villages were held in thrall by one or more missionary churches. In my time in Nome, a dozen or more (they came and went) missionary churches fought with great skill over the two thousand or so Eskimos that were children of God and not too far from being pure primitives.

From time to time the administrators of these religious organizations in the South 48 would decide it was time to visit the northern hinterlands, and with collection plates overflowing from months or years of children and others dropping their nickels and dimes into them, a trip would be laid on. From my experience with missionaries in bush Alaska, they had a good thing going and didn't want it mucked up by nosy administrators poking around their village. Often bad weather would trap a visiting party of church noblemen for a week or more, wreaking havoc or hell on the missionary larder and social life.

Almost all missionaries were drawn from the lower classes of devoted church workers. Accepting an assignment to the wilds of Alaska made them heroes in the eyes of the brethren. Once out of sight of the mother mission, these adventurous people, usually a husband and wife with perhaps a child or two, all Bible-thumpers of the first water, would realize they could fairly well write their own ticket up north, and most chose to live a lifestyle well above what they would have attained back in West Virginia or Arkansas or the eastern piney hills of Texas. Once they learned the system, they soon acquired the skill of asking for more and better. Often this included maid service and paid help to haul water and collect firewood.

ONE OF THE MOST REMARKABLE FLIGHTS ever made by Don Sheldon was a mission school and church inspection trip for three Ohio church administrators who wanted to see both how the nickels and dimes were being spent and as much of Alaska as they could get in.

Don picked up these business-suited men at Anchorage. He liked to fly into Merrill Field, check the shops for Cessna and Piper parts, and scoot back with a load of passengers who would base themselves in Talkeetna. The churchmen would be asked to put up at Evil Alice's Talkeetna Motel or at the Fairview Inn, both centers of social intercourse after the dinner hour where the normal clientele was a cross-section of Alaska's bush types: hard drinkers, noisy dancers, and the kind who would send squat bottles of Oly down to your place at the bar if you made any conversation at all. Everyone sat at the bar.

A circle of two hundred miles or so around Talkeetna would take in much of Alaska, and in the case of the three visiting churchmen encompassed the four mission churches for which they were responsible. The circle also touched Fairbanks and enfolded Denali National Park on the north and extended almost to the end of the Kenai Peninsula and the edge of the Wrangell Mountain wilderness to the south.

I won't mention the year, or the places visited by these

church functionaries, as my purpose is not to humiliate or ridicule anyone. Alaska is a most democratic state, and almost anything goes. A man is better judged on how he holds his fly rod than by anything he can show in his past as good works.

Sheldon had to ground his Ohioans in Talkeetna after the run up from Anchorage because of poor weather, but he had them where he could gather them up and be gone in minutes, once the atmosphere cleared. In the meantime, Don continued making hauls to places he could get in and out of safely. When the sky finally cleared to the north, he loaded the men into the Cessna that was fourteen pounds lighter than similar planes because he left it unpainted. During the long well-lit hours of this particular day, Don moved the churchmen from village to village, always via some great spectacle like Mount McKinley gleaming up over the clouds or the striped backs of the glaciers flowing down from the giant mountain.

Don would putter around the airplane while the churchmen made their visit. He would be offered lunch or lemonade by a missionary wife, but he usually kept to himself, often catching an hour or so of sleep in some shady spot near the plane. He had quoted them a flat figure for the whole trip, and on this day, he thought he would be able to touch all the bases and be back home for dinner with his wife, Roberta, and the kids.

After the last visit, one of the churchmen told Don that they were soon to leave Alaska and hadn't seen one wild animal. Most pilots of small planes were keenly interested in giving passengers from the Outside a look at Alaska's big bears, moose, or caribou. Or they would strive to show off a Dall sheep group or mountain goat family. The pilots were as proud of the Great Land's bounty as any other

Alaskan. So Don said he would see what he could do about delivering Alaska's famous wildlife before he took them all back to Talkeetna.

Soon they were seeing giant moose browsing in the muskeg near the Kuskokwim River. Don told the men that these old-timers had "six-foot wingspans," and he flew low over the feeding bulls to make sure everyone agreed on the distance from one antler tip to the other.

Don spotted a blonde grizzly with cub in a stream ahead. "Toklat griz, a little south of its stamping grounds," he yelled, and put the silver plane into another vertical bank so that all the cameras could click. This time the griz, her yellow fur dripping wet, clawed the air to keep the Cessna from bothering the cub, now safely on the far bank.

Don lucked out when he took a shortcut over a no-name mountain and found the valley on the far side filled with "wall-to-wall caribou." The fantastic antlers were undulating in the low sunlight as the herd moved through the pass. Don saw a clearing and put the Cessna down, much to the surprise of the passengers, who thought twenty feet above the herd was close enough.

"Everybody out," he told them. "You'll get some great photos if you stay near the plane." Moments later, the curious caribou streamed past the Cessna, close enough to enable the Easterners to feel their hair as they ran by. All the cameras were empty when Don loaded the church-men back aboard and headed the silver plane into the wind.

THE BUMPY TAKEOFF was more than a bit of bush field inconvenience. It concealed the fact that a bungee cord that held the front tip of a landing ski in position had broken. The skis were long, wide skids that permitted the airplane to land on both snow and ice. With a bungee or rubber cable at each end, the skis were held ready for the snow. The bungees offered flexibility when running on snow, keeping the tips up.

With the right-front bungee broken and the plane in the air, there was a grave situation that could mean a possibly deadly crash on landing. The ski, now flying flat against the slipstream and held that way by the rear bungee, was making the plane very unstable. Don had to keep full power on, causing the plane to roar as if in a permanent takeoff. Staying aloft was becoming problematical.

Don, not wanting to add alarm to the bad situation, turned around to look at the passengers and told them, "Gentlemen, we are going too slow to fly and too fast to crash. We will not be able to land unless we can get the ski down. How about you" — and he pointed to the man seated next to the right-hand door in the backseat — "getting out on the tail of the ski."

This order met with dumb looks. But Don poked around with his free hand, found an end of a mountaineering rope, and told the unhappy prospect to tie the rope around his waist. Don told the man to zip up his jacket and put on his gloves, he was going out to counterbalance the errant ski. The other passengers held on to their partner as he pushed his legs out the door, fighting the slipstream. Don tied the other end of the rope to a seat belt, hoping its strength would not have to be tested.

Luckily the man had galoshes on to protect his feet and lower legs, and the partially closed door sheltered most of him from the icy slipstream. He was now partway in and partway out of the plane. He floundered around with his feet until he found the edge of the ski tail and then, lowering his weight, he slowly brought the tip down to near horizontal. The Cessna immediately began to fly better, and all aboard realized that the sacrifice in comfort had to be made for all their safety.

I'm sure the churchmen now expected Don to find an airfield and land, repair the broken bungee, and proceed in the normal way. But Don felt it was best to make tracks for home base in Talkeetna. He was not certain what would happen when he set the plane down with the man on the ski tail, so he preferred to be on home ground when they met Mother Earth. In retrospect he was right, but the fellow on the ski tail could not be relieved, and he hung there, partially in and partially out of the plane, for nearly ninety minutes while Don raced for home.

He radioed in from a few miles out, asking Roberta to meet the plane with a fire extinguisher. She was waiting at the end of the airstrip that runs by the Sheldon home, holding the red carbon dioxide extinguisher tank and wondering what to expect, when the Cessna whooshed by her with a fellow hanging half out of the cabin.

The plane settled firmly to the airstrip on its skis, and the horror of balancing the ski tip was over. The nearly frozen passenger was soon thawed. Alice said everyone did justice to the pitcher of hot buttered rum she quickly cooked up—all except Don, who went home and about his business as if nothing had happened. ✈

Chapter 8

Bringing 'Em
Back Alive _____

Don Sheldon was so highly skilled with both ski and wheel
planes that it was hard to remember he was perhaps even
better on floats with a loaded plane. *Time* magazine hired
him to take me and an editor to the mouth of the Yukon
River on an assignment one weekend—to a place named
Eek.

I doubt if he had been there more than once, if at all,
as it is not what you would call a popular place to visit.
And it was, at that time of year, half under water. But
Don landed the floatplane, got us onto the shore,
unloaded my photo gear, and then left to refuel at Bethel.

I didn't finish my assignment of taking photos of
children's primitive artwork until near dark. We were sure
that Don would never find the place again—and even if
he did, he wouldn't be able to land, with the Eek River
rushing by in the dark. But he found the place and did a
perfect job of landing. We loaded, took off, set down in
Bethel for dinner, and then took off for Talkeetna. The *Time*
editor, a guy named Jesse Birnbaum, was up front with
Don. I was in the back seat, jammed in with photo gear
and some freight Don had picked up in Bethel.

Once we reached about 8,000 feet, Don asked Birnbaum
if he had ever done any flying. Yes, he said, he had been

an engineer on a B-24 bomber during the war and had twenty-five combat missions under his belt.

"Well, you got about as much experience as I have," Don said, "so how about taking the controls while I catch some shut-eye?" The dual controls were presented to Birnbaum.

"Keep an eye on this guy, Joe," Don said to me, "and when you see a bright light on the far right, wake me up—that will be Skwentna." And Don curled up and went to sleep. He snored while the editor from New York City, who told me later he had never even taxied a B-24 much less piloted one, held the control column and kept a certain black mountain range on the horizon.

Don slept on as Birnbaum drove the floatplane through the air, muttering to himself, "They'd never believe this in the office. Me flying across Alaska at night!"

By craning my neck, I finally found a weak light down below in the dark, a light that kept getting stronger. I shook Don.

"Nope, that's Farewell, but it's time to take us through the Range."

Below us were the headwaters of the Kuskokwim River and the tail end of the Alaska Range. Straight ahead I could see jagged peaks gleaming against the night sky. Don stretched himself like the big cat that he was and sat up. There was an elaborate stretching of the legs and rubbing of the eyes, and a look all around into the darkness. Birnbaum was happy to relinquish his role as pilot.

We all could see the solid wall of ice and snow coming at us, but Don continued with his waking-up process. Birnbaum was afraid that Don hadn't seen the mountains ahead and pointed in fear.

"Oh yeah," Don said, "that's Mount Dall with 9,000

feet of rocks and ice waiting for us. Better get around it as we only got 8,000 ourselves." With a sure hand, he flew around the white eminence.

"Hey, Birnbaum, you did all right! How about takin' it for another ten minutes or so while I get the rest of these cobwebs swept out?" And Don curled up into his sleep position again and was gone. Perhaps this was the secret of Don's ability to fly those twenty-hour days and nights.

Birnbaum was now a bit more confident, but he said in a loud voice that Don was certain to hear, "I don't know why *Time* has to pay for all this flying when I'm doing it myself!"

Don didn't move. Soon, down on the right, I saw the bright light of Skwentna and woke Don. He was all business now.

"Hey, I'm going to sign you off as an Alaska floatplane pilot. You did a helluva job bringing us in from Bethel," he yelled at Birnbaum.

Don cracked open one of the vents, and a cold stream of night air fresh from the flanks of McKinley swept all the sleep out of us.

We were above the Susitna River, heading toward Don's home base of Talkeetna, but I couldn't see enough to tell where we were.

"Hey, Birnbaum," Don yelled, "as soon as I get her down, get out on the float and grab that branch as we go by. The current will have us down to Anchorage if you don't!"

I'm certain Birnbaum had no idea where we were. He only knew we were heading downhill on a path of air. All of a sudden we heard the smooth splash of the floats cutting the river water, the engine rev up, and a yell from Don: "OK, get out and grab!"

We heard the scrape of a branch along the side of the plane, and then Birnbaum yelled, "I got it!" Don cut the engine and got out a flashlight. He had the plane tied up safe and snug, the gear in the plane unloaded into his Jeep, and us on our way to a bed at Evil Alice's Talkeetna Motel before we knew it.

"Joe, I don't believe what we just did," Birnbaum said. "I think I need a drink!" We dumped our stuff into our rooms and went to the bar. A feeble light shone over the bar, and Alice was cleaning up the last of the bar trash.

"Scotch and water—doubles," Birnbaum told her.

"Sorry, honey, the bar's closed, but there's no good reason you can't help yourself," she said, and walked out saying "good night." I remember the bottle of Peter Dawson that first came to hand—it was a tad more than half full, but in fifteen minutes it was empty.

ON AN ASSIGNMENT in the Brooks Range in northern Alaska in 1969, our crew was desperate to find some "wolf action"—scenes of real wolves tearing into wild flesh or chasing down some game—to use in the NBC-TV production "The Wolf Men." I was working with John Alonzo, who went on to become one of Hollywood's greater cameramen and location directors. Don Sheldon was our pilot in pursuit of wolves to film.

While refueling one of the Cessnas at the airfield at Bettles, we ran into Bill Bacon, the wonderful wildlife cinematographer for Disney. I'd known Bill for years, as Disney would send him up from his home in Sequim, Washington, from time to time, and he'd always get in touch with me for information or just to be friendly. He asked what we were doing up north, and I told him about our wolf search.

"You're not trying to film real live wild wolves, are you?" he asked. I told him that was the assignment.

He muttered something about our sanity. "You'll be here a long time before you even see one, and then getting a wolf to do anything filmworthy will be another wait," he told me.

"What does Disney use when he needs wild wolves?" I asked.

"We locate a pack of malamute or husky sled dogs that someone is raising in the bush, and then dip them in a case of Lady Clairol to make them wolf-looking," he told me with a wink. "At least they respond to some commands."

But we were sworn to using real wolves only—and Don Sheldon and his number-two pilot Mike Fisher, with the help of an ace wolf hunter, were going to find us some if it took until the snow melted.

Flying out of Chandalar in iffy weather the next morning in the Piper Super Cub, Don spotted a moving caribou herd. He and John Alonzo were in the plane, a ski-equipped performer that was ideal for taking aerial animal films because of the wide-open side doors. With a light snowfall and caribou ahead as far as he could see, Don told Alonzo to get ready to film because they were bound to see wolves nibbling on the caribou herd. Sure enough, they found a pack of a dozen wolves working the northeast corner of the herd, and Don quickly brought the plane down close to the ground.

I was in the Cessna with Mike, shooting still photos for promotional use and for a possible related article. Mike had the Cessna up about 500 feet, and I could see Don's red-and-yellow Super Cub down among the trees, with caribou ahead. We couldn't see the wolves, so Mike took

the faster plane down lower. But then a warning from Don put us back up a bit as he didn't want to spook the wolves.

Don finally got his plane lined up on a strung-out pack of wolves racing through the fresh snow, steam pouring from their mouths as they ran. Ahead was the vague form of the snowy caribou herd, just becoming aware that wolves were attacking.

Don put the plane lower until it was flying between trees and the prop wash was kicking up a spume of snow. I couldn't tell what was happening. But somewhere on this slow tail-chase, Don lost control of the plane. It wobbled—and I could see a crash coming if something didn't change soon.

Later we learned the whole story. Don, looking over his left shoulder, had seen to his horror that Alonzo was no longer in the backseat. The enthusiastic cameraman had run one magazine of film through the Eclair camera, shooting through the prop arc of the propeller. But he knew he could get better pictures by leaving the cockpit and sliding out onto the wing strut until he was clear of the prop arc and could get a rare, unobstructed view of wolves and caribou.

Don pulled at the ankle end of Alonzo's insulated one-piece snowmobile suit, getting him to look over toward the cockpit. "Mr. Alonzo," he said, in a replay of his words to the Ohio churchmen, "We are going too slow to fly and too fast to crash; come back into the cockpit!"

Alonzo looked ahead, then at his film magazine to see how many more feet of film he had, and waved at Don to go ahead and fly. This wobbling aircraft was an accident waiting to happen, and Mike and I had our fingers crossed as we watched. John was out on the strut, obstructing the prop wash from flowing over the tail and rudder and reducing Don's ability to steer the little plane. Finally they zoomed over the herd and Alonzo gave Don the OK sign and crawled back into the Cub's cockpit. Don took the plane up, and we joined them at 500 feet.

"He's out of film," Don radioed to Mike. Mike told me that was the nicest news we had all morning. We made it back to Red Adney's lodge on Chandalar. After taking off his layers of clothing and lacing himself with some brandy-fortified coffee, Alonzo described what turned out to be the best wolf/caribou movies ever made.

When I saw the takes later, I saw fantastic close-cropped action of snow flying off the feet of racing wolves, their faces belching steam—and within that same scene, caribou running for their lives. It was very fine photography that only Alonzo's daredevil air tactic could have produced. The wolf-chase footage was the highlight of the one-hour TV special. ✈

Chapter 9

Snow Job _____

We once hauled two BP Oil Company advertising executives from London around parts of Alaska as they scanned locations for TV commercials featuring the company's new gas pump and logo. I was hired to make color photos of each location. Don Sheldon warned the execs to dress warmly for the flight, but sure enough, they got to the Talkeetna strip wearing Saville Row lightweight clothing. There was no time to find warmer clothing, but they insisted they would be "just fine." Sure—as long as there were no sudden stops between Talkeetna and Talkeetna.

We flew into and out of almost every glacier valley around Mount McKinley: the Buckskin, the Muldrow, the Kahiltna, and of course the mighty Ruth. The canyon of the Ruth Glacier rivals the Grand Canyon, except that 5,000 feet of its 10,000-foot depth is filled with snow and ice.

The Ruth offered everything the advertising script asked for, and the men insisted we land and make a series of color photos. Don could see a good thing coming: dozens of shuttles onto the glacier with loads of gear to make the TV ads. But the glacier surface looked a bit too fresh for me, and Don had some qualms about putting the Cessna down on that unmarked white surface.

"Give me my lunch bag," Don told one of the men

sitting behind him, and a wrinkled brown paper bag containing the remains of his lunch was passed up to him. He needed something heavy to put in the bag, so I handed him a full can of Coke. He headed the plane down to the end of the glacier where he wanted to land, made a steep turn, and tossed the bag out the window.

"Keep an eye on that thing, Joe," he told me as he circled for another look. None of us could spot the brown bag on the white snow surface a hundred feet below us.

"Give me my zipper bag behind the back seat," Don demanded. It was passed up as he flew back to the end of the glacier.

I knew what Don was up to. I had gone through this drill before with both Don and Mike Fisher, his number-two pilot. Toss something fairly heavy out of the plane, and if it disappears under the snow, you just don't land. Fresh, fluffy, mountain-generated powder snow will not support an airplane. The stuff can pile up over twenty feet deep.

Don dropped the airline bag out of the window, and we lost it almost immediately. I guess Don's eyes were filled with dollar signs, because he never made the slightest comment as he maneuvered the Cessna on skis into position to land on the snow.

DON MADE A PERFECT LANDING, though we were completely blinded by blowing snow. He gunned the engine before we lost forward movement and was successful in getting the plane to turn in the snow and point back down the glacier. Then the engine stopped, and we found ourselves buried in feathery snowflakes. Later we measured seven feet of snow above the wing!

The doors were blocked by snow and couldn't be

opened. I managed to ram the door open on the right side and get out. The snowflakes had the consistency of feathers, with enough space between to allow me to breathe. I made my way to the wing strut, untied the snowshoes, and shoveled a "cave" for me to work in. Soon I had worked through the roof of snowflakes and saw the plight we were in.

Wearing the snowshoes, I stomped a path to the front of the plane, and Don was able to get out on his side. He cleared the snow from the front of the plane and from the wings. I then made a wide path from the front of the plane to the surface of the snowdrift, and I could see that we were perfectly hidden beneath the snow surface.

Don had put on the other pair of snowshoes, telling the two executives that there was "no problem." He told me to stomp a path down the glacier for five hundred yards or so and to keep packing it down until he said to quit.

Don's plan was to stomp a hardened route up from the depths of the snowdrift and onto the surface and to then fly the airplane out, with just himself aboard to lighten the load. With the two of us stomping and packing, we made a path, none too straight, across the glacier top. The Ruth is so huge that we were playing in just a small part of what Don called the upper amphitheater.

The two ad men were soon shivering in their street clothes, and I told them to help us by putting their London oxfords to work packing a hard snow path for the plane as it emerged from the depths. If the route wasn't packed enough, the plane would bury itself again. They didn't think the situation was funny, nor did they wish to be used as day laborers. I told them it was a matter of life or death—theirs—because they wouldn't survive the night the way they were dressed, and I wasn't apt to give up my down parka and long johns.

I always carried a pocket-full of hard candies wrapped in cellophane, so I passed some around. Don made it clear we were not to toss the wrappers around; this was sacred ground to him.

We sucked the candies, and we stomped, and when the path looked good enough for a freeway to freedom, Don got in the plane and prepared for flight. I told him to call his wife, Roberta, when he got the engine turning so that we could count on a helicopter rescue from Talkeetna for the two Londoners, if not for us. But he was confident we would be able to fly out.

With full power on and the whole back of the plane shaking off the fluffy snow, the Cessna surged up onto the hardened path. But Don could not hold it there. There are no brakes on the ski-equipped Cessna. It has inertia, and moves until friction or another force stops it. The Cessna lurched forward, with Don trying to steer it, but ran off the track into another burial plot. We had to dig Don out, then the plane.

Our second attempt was easier because we already had experience building the path and had the rhythm for stomping. One of the Londoners tried to put on Don's snowshoes, but they didn't attach well to his low-quarter street shoes. Both men complained of being cold. Don dug out the quilted nylon engine cover, and I made a seat for the men and wrapped them in the engine cover. Don had not made a call to Roberta or to anyone else to report our plight.

While stomping out an escape path for the second time, it dawned on me that Don's nemesis at this time, the late '60s, was the helicopter! If word got out that he had to

have chopper rescue for his passengers and himself, he would lose face! It would be a concession that his mountain kingdom was really a place for helicopter service, not for his fixed-wing planes.

Don got back into the cockpit without comment for the second attempt. We three watched while the bird roared, huffed and puffed, shook off its powder snow load, and after twenty or so feet of staying on the straight and narrow, again fell off the hard path into deep powder snow.

To make this snow job less of a chore to relate, I will shorten it by saying we stomped five paths from the five graves the plane settled into that afternoon. By that time, the sun was getting low, with a chill sinking down on us as our options were running out. The smallest of the men complained of pains in his upper arm and side—a sure sign of angina, I thought, and he had left his pills at the motel in Talkeetna.

I quickly finished the sixth runway and did a better than average job on the ramp up from the plane's ski tips to the glacier surface. I told Don that I was afraid one of the men shivering in the greasy engine-cowl blanket was having a heart attack and that we had to get him out. I demanded he call Roberta or anyone else for help. Even a helicopter would take thirty to sixty minutes to get to us, and the sun was leaving those long shadows that make great pictures but dim the prospects for rescue.

DON SLAMMED THE PLANE'S DOOR and faked a call to Roberta. Standing on the step, I could see that his finger wasn't pushing the mike switch.

I moved the men behind the plane and told Don he had one more chance to make it. We had worked for hours packing the glacier freeway system, and we had no more hours left. I told Don that if he didn't call for helicopter rescue, I would henceforth cease being his friend and his very important flying customer. He yelled to me to bring the sick man to the plane. I helped the fellow to the right-hand door, pushed him up into the seat, buckled him in, and covered him with a blanket.

The engine roared with life as Don poured the maximum fuel to it. The plane lurched from its snowy grave and hobbled up onto the hardened track for about fifty feet, but as it started to pick up speed, it fell off the track and into the deep snow. But it kept on going! With the engine roaring wide open, the bulging snow gave way as the Cessna plowed through at least a quarter mile of drift, leaped across a crevasse, and rode the surface snow to a spectacular takeoff, showering snowflakes for half a mile.

They were off. I figured Don would report he had left two men behind on the glacier, without specifically asking for a helicopter rescue. People would understand the implication that unless the Good Lord—or a chopper—reached out a hand to us soon, we would not get out that night, or perhaps ever.

Well, it was a fantastic location in which to die. The towering McKinley massif across our northern horizon and the peaks that flank the amphitheater all reflected the golden glow of sunset. The Londoner and I sat on the cowl cover and discussed our chances of getting out alive.

I told him our chances were 100 percent better than before, now that the Cessna had broken free. But how long would it be until rescue? I said that if there was no helicopter at Talkeetna, one coming from Anchorage would be at least an hour en route. At that moment, an Alaska Airlines plane headed for Fairbanks flew by and banked a little to allow its passengers to witness the two idiots on the Ruth Glacier. We had become news as the FAA had made us an advisory item. I assumed a chopper would be up soon.

Surprise! Don was back, making a low pass over us. Just behind him was a Bell helicopter making its approach. We were soon aboard the roomy whirlybird. I was out of film, but as we flew away, I would have given an entire camera to have just one more frame of film so that I could show the Ruth Glacier with all our hardened paths embossed on its otherwise pristine surface as it showed its best face in the late golden light.

Alice Powell met the chopper with some hot buttered rum, and the Londoner revived quickly. The sick fellow had rosy cheeks now, so he and his partner immediately hired the chopper for a direct flight to Merrill Field in

Anchorage, where they ordered a cab to the Captain Cook Hotel.

Back in Talkeetna, all I got from Charles Towill, the BP public relations man, was an order to keep Don Sheldon as far away from BP as I could. He told me to consider myself on short time as a location adviser if I used such bad judgment again.

After loading up with a large T-bone from Alice's VIP locker and a bottle of Louis Martini zinfandel that she had dug up somewhere, I crawled into my motel bed at 9 P.M. and slept till noon. ✈

Chapter 10

The Enemy _____

Don Sheldon hated whirlybirds with a passion. He resented their intrusion upon his kingdom of mountains and glaciers. And he realized that a helicopter could do everything that he could accomplish with a single-engine plane—and do it better, in most cases, because it could hover and land on a few square feet of ice, snow, or rock.

After a helicopter once parked near Don's refueling area on the Talkeetna village strip, he spotted it when he got home at night from eighteen hours of flying. Tired as he was, Don was up watching the whirlybird early next morning, a teacup in his hand, when the pilot emerged from one of the hotels to begin his day's work. Don was on him in a flash. Don told the pilot that his wife did not hang up a load of wet laundry in order to have a "hilleycopter" paste it with flying mud and dirt. He said he had three small children in a fenced yard next to the village strip, and he didn't want them hurt by flying debris kicked up by the bird. That afternoon, the chopper was down for the night at Evil Alice's, a quarter mile away. Don had made his point.

But what he feared was inevitable. The Vietnam War had produced thousands of helicopter pilots, just as the Korean War and World War II had produced and turned loose thousands of competent fixed-wing pilots. The technological age had come to Alaska, and the helicopter, for those who could afford it, was king.

The helicopter's ability to go almost anywhere made it a natural for photographic missions. For films and video, it reigned supreme because the vibration caused by the rotary wings was never noticed in the film, especially when accessories like the Kenyon Stabilizer were used to dampen the movement of cameras. The high cost placed the chopper in only a few hands, but those users usually came up with superior results.

THE HELICOPTER PLAYED A PART in an environmental minidrama I witnessed while on assignment for the National Geographic Society. We were again based in wonderful downtown Talkeetna. National Geographic was an outfit that could afford the best camera platform, so it had hired a helicopter to whisk its people around the state. This time it was the books division of National Geographic that was picking up the tab, and it had assigned a typical team of writer, photographer, and editor to the project.

I wasn't the project photographer. I was simply hired to do a few days of photo coverage of the editor at work, and perhaps of the photographer, for publicity purposes. These pictures would help announce the new book and show how it was produced.

One morning I flew out with the editor and—not untypically, being so far from the home office—his girlfriend, with whom he was touring. Two can live as cheaply as one, as long as the accounting is massaged and reheated enough before submission for reimbursement to National Geographic.

We had a beautiful day, a two-hundred-dollar-an-hour whirlybird, and two people in love who wanted to see the heart of Alaska. I was behind their seat with my wide-angle Nikon, asked to keep the female clear of any shots that would go to headquarters for editing. I knew the country intimately from many trips with Don Sheldon and Mike Fisher, so I suggested a flight path to start. We would go one way until noon, return to Evil Alice's wonderful board for lunch and a quickie nap, and then catch the afternoon light and eventide from the lofty perch of the bird.

We flitted from one great place to another on our magic carpet. Starting into Denali National Park from the southern foothills and front ranges that protect the giant three—McKinley, Foraker, and Hunter—we swooped from viewpoint to viewpoint coming into this legendary region. By about 11:30, we had covered more high ground and saw more fantastic scenery than any previous explorer or mountaineer, effortlessly.

THE PILOT HAD PICKED OUT a superb place to stop for a last view before our lunch break. High up on a small point at the top of a 10,000-foot mountain—too low for climbers and too high for the casual trekker—was a spot about the size of a parking space. The landing gear of the Bell helicopter allowed just enough room around the front three sides for us to stand in awe as we perched 7,500 feet above the Kahiltna Glacier, row after row of smaller peaks behind us. It was truly an eagle's nest. I quickly went through a roll of film.

As we looked at the view in amazement and noted the great mountains now appearing out of the clouds, the girl-friend took a large Hershey bar from her parka pocket and proceeded to do a terrible thing. She removed the dark

brown paper and then the foil around the chocolate and
threw the debris onto the ground.

The pilot exploded in a frenzy. At first I couldn't imagine what had triggered his outburst. He pointed to the
torn bits of wrapper on the sacred ground of our lookout
and cursed her like I've heard few people cursed before.
He told her to get on her knees and pick up her "shit" and
then get back in the helicopter and stay there. He told her
boyfriend that she was now persona non grata, a person
who should be deported from the Great Land for her vile
Eastern ways.

We all got back in the helicopter. The pilot revved up
the bird and powered it over the edge. In a suicidal drop
I've never experienced before or since, he let the chopper
fall thousands of feet, nearly to the glacier floor, before
whipping it about and heading back to Talkeetna. Our
tour was over. ✦

Chapter 11

Peak Excitement  _____

When Alaska statehood came in 1959, a great new interest was created in Alaska's high peaks, and Bradford Washburn became one of Don Sheldon's best customers. Brad used the roof of Alaska as his playground, climbing everything that poked up into the clear blue sky. His wife, Barbara, climbed Mount McKinley with him, becoming the first woman to reach the summit. Washburn spent much time exploring the peaks, and he photographed several Switzerlands' worth of beauty and majesty. The take appeared in magazines such as *Life* and *National Geographic* and in scientific journals.

Washburn wasn't alone. Mountaineers from around the world wanted to add McKinley and other peaks of the Alaska Range to their lists of conquests, and Don Sheldon was the key to the glacier base camps. He flew up and down the Ruth and Kahiltna glaciers as if they were his own. Sheldon and Mount McKinley were one.

A WINTER CLIMB OF MOUNT MCKINLEY had been considered for many years, and in 1966 plans were made to assault the ice tower the following January. The expedition under leadership of mountaineer Gregg Blomberg was staffed with both local and international alpinists such as Ray Genet, Art Davidson, and Shiro Nashimae. Planning included elaborate testing by the Institute of Arctic Biology of the University of Alaska, with hopes of pointing out body changes caused by the ordeal.

This attempt at a first winter climb grabbed the interest of the folks at *Time* and *Life* magazines, mainly through my efforts at pumping up its potential importance. I was assigned full time to the photo coverage, and Jordan Bonfante, just back from a stint in Rome for *Life*, was sent up from Los Angeles to take charge of the project.

I'll never forget the initial flight with Jordan to the Kahiltna Glacier, when Don Sheldon flew us in his silver Cessna, loaded to the windows with gear and supplies he intended to dump off at the climbers' base camp. Don was at the top of his form with this chance to show a newcomer the realities of bush flying.

Don asked me to squirm into a spot in the plane where normally the rear seat would be. Then he jammed Jordan in front of me, with my knees serving as a back rest. Neither of us could see out the wide windows unless Don banked the Cessna almost on its wingtip. The cockpit was jammed full.

Neither Jordan nor I had safety belts. The belts wouldn't work without the seats, and the seats had been taken out to make room for the cargo. Don told Jordan it was this way or not at all. We made the best of it, Jordan in his Los Angeles sports coat and slacks over the down long johns I made him put on. I pinned my Eddie Bauer mountaineering gloves to his coat sleeves.

Don started the takeoff from the backyard of his home. As the ski plane gained speed and bounced along the snow-covered strip, Jordan gave me a game thumbs-up.

Just as he did, the right-hand door popped open and he and some of the gear nearly fell out. Don casually reached across Jordan's cringing body and slammed the door shut. He made some remark about the plane being too full.

Heading toward the foothills of the national park, Don said he had to change his footwear. He put his head under the instrument panel and carefully unzipped one rubber galosh and pulled his left foot out. He gave the foot an airing as he searched around for his mukluks, which were in a bag somewhere under his seat. Then he bent down below the instrument panel again, straightening out his heavy woolen socks and slipping his foot into the mukluk. He wiggled his foot and finally tied the elaborate red-tasseled laces.

All this time, Don had not looked out the windshield or the side window, but more or less kept a conversation going with Jordan, who had screwed himself deeper into the gear to find bottom and brace himself better. I felt him thrust up against my knees and noticed his look of hopelessness as we charged through the air at 120 miles per hour with apparently no one driving the silver coffin.

With one mukluk on and in partial comfort, Don went through the whole procedure with the right foot, then gave us all a big Wyoming Boy smile when he was rebooted and warm. The plane was now well over the foothills and I could see, from time to time, the jagged extensions of McKinley and her neighbor, Mount Foraker.

At this point, we appeared to be headed for a solid wall of ice and snow. Finally Jordan could stand it no longer. He looked over his shoulder at me with pleading eyes and whispered, "Are you sure this is the best pilot to get us up to base camp?"

"Jordan," I whispered back, "this is the only pilot to

get us to base camp, and back. Relax!"

Don put the Cessna into a steep bank to the left. We could see, only too well, the rocky and icy ridge below us as we threaded an opening between the rocks. Then down we went in a steep dive, Don pointing out the camp far below on the glacier.

Planes from other news organizations were already flying around the snowy bowl. Don said he would have to clear some air space for us.

Over the radio, we heard the other planes debating their rights. We could hear "red plane" telling "blue plane" to get out of the way so that CBS News could get a clear shot of the camp. "Blue plane" came back with some obscenity and said NBC-TV had as much right to be in the national park sky as CBS. Don jumped in.

"One-seven-four Yankee, carrying the *Life* magazine team, will be landing at base camp if you fellas will give me some elbow room," he said. We saw the other news planes pull up. Don did one of his fancy steep banks, sideslipped a bit, and had the Cessna down on the glacier's packed snow as slick as a whistle. Jordan gave me another thumbs-up.

We taxied up to the camp, and Don turned the silver plane around to point downhill for a fast takeoff in case the weather turned sour. Walking around to the right-hand door, Don turned the handle and Jordan fell out.

"Welcome to Kahiltna Glacier," Don said.

ONE OF THE OTHER PEOPLE who showed Sheldon how to attack the land of ice and snow was a mountaineering educator named Terris Moore, former president of the University of Alaska and a climbing friend of Brad Washburn's.

I didn't meet Moore until 1968, when I was attached to the Mount Kennedy/Southwest Yukon Expedition carried out by the National Geographic Society on the Hubbard Glacier in Canada's Yukon Territory.

The expedition itself didn't have an airplane, so a flying service from Whitehorse helped move us about. This outfit's Beaver on skis was a bit unwieldy, but until we started to attack the mountains immediately by Mount Kennedy, we didn't need a very light plane.

Terry Moore, bored with retirement, decided to join us out on the Hubbard. He flew his souped-up, redesigned Piper Super Cub out from Cambridge, Massachusetts. We got a wire every morning from Terry, relayed by the Whitehorse bush pilot, telling us that he was here or there, beset or pushed by good weather and approaching our lair at the rate of several hundred miles a day.

Terry landed his red-and-white Cub on the glacier, right in front of our camp. He had made it to our Hubbard Glacier camp in six flying days, and as soon as he had some lunch, he was ready to haul me to the top of a 10,000-foot ridge to help set up a surveying position for triangulation of Mount Kennedy.

The big fuss over Mount Kennedy developed after the Canadian government began to name some of the 13,000-foot peaks in the range. Unexpectedly, the idea of honoring the late President Kennedy by naming a mountain for him generated a lot of interest. So the knob that had been known as East Hubbard Peak became Mount Kennedy.

It was deemed imperative that a member of the Kennedy family make the first ascent. I suggested Rose, but no one listened.

Four Canadian parties had requested permission to climb the peak before it got the Kennedy name, but they were pushed aside by the government because of pressure from Washington to allow Robert Kennedy to climb it first. Of course, Kennedy was no mountaineer, but his political organization included the mountaineering Whittaker brothers of Washington state. In 1963, Jim Whittaker had become the first American to climb Mount Everest. They were urged to put together a team of climbers to get Robert Kennedy to the top of the new Mount Kennedy while the world's press clicked away.

The climb itself wasn't much, and it didn't reflect a bit of credit on either Robert Kennedy or mountaineering. The sponsoring National Geographic Society sort of ignored the whole thing, simply wrapping the climb into its ongoing and long-planned Southwest Yukon mapping expedition under Washburn and Maynard Miller. The *National Geographic* magazine never ran a story on the so-called Mount Kennedy climb, and editor Bill Garrett said it would be a cold day in hell before it did.

The mapping expedition did great work, however, and turned out a first-class map of the region. It marked an important effort to correct some of the problems with the old system of using prominent peaks along the border of Alaska and the Yukon Territory to mark separation of the United States and Canada.

One wag had his own way of explaining the border situation: "Most of the people who come up here think that Alaska belongs to Canada, and they carry passports and other such I.D. But it is well known by the remainder that the Yukon is actually part of Alaska, which is part of the Uppa U.S."

Of course, Alaska had become a state by that time, so we figured the confusion would sort itself out in a few generations. ✦

Chapter 12

Lifesaver _____

Don Sheldon saved my life once in a maneuver that had all the makings of a Charlie Chaplin comedy, although I wasn't awake to enjoy it. It was an occasion that found me near death—a big negative number for judgment on my part, but part of the calculated risk one takes when everything seems to be OK but really isn't.

The occasion for my near-death experience was that expedition to make the first winter climb of McKinley. Covering the affair for *Time* and *Life,* I had almost carte blanche on expenses. With both magazines splitting the costs, Jordan Bonfante and I had the money to lay on more air coverage. We especially wanted to show climbers ascending a high ridge on the mountain.

Don Sheldon felt his Cessna was not the right machine for the job and that this high-altitude photo mission needed another aircraft. Jordan gave me the OK to hire a special photo plane to take me up into the ridges surrounding McKinley's summit. I told Don to order up the airplane he thought we would need—as long as he was able to fly it. I didn't want some greenhorn trying to learn about mountain flying with me hanging out of the plane.

Don flew down to Anchorage and tried out a Turbo Beaver single-engine ski plane from SeaAirMotive. He had them remove the rear cargo door and cover the bottom half of the opening with a piece of three-quarter-inch plywood. I put an old mattress on the floor, planning to kneel on the mattress and shoot my pictures over the top of the plywood windscreen. Don said it would be terribly cold up at 17,000 and 18,000 feet, but he knew I couldn't take a chance on trying to get decent shots through a frosty window. The front cabin windows offered a very limited range of visibility and plenty of strut and wing obstruction.

We waited two days for a clearing weather pattern and a radio call from the team making its way up from the igloos they had built at 14,400 feet, around from the part of the mountain known as Windy Corner. The climbers were making good progress up a rocky ridge at 17,200 feet. The setting would be perfect for a picture with the summit behind them to the east.

Climber Art Davidson was asked what he would like most, and he said a glass of grapefruit juice! The climbers were all feeling dehydrated from the exertion and the altitude. I went to the Talkeetna Trading Post and bought up all the bags of grapefruits and oranges I could find. If my memory serves me, I had six netted sacks of grapefruit and six of large navel oranges plus some six-packs of fruit drinks double-wrapped in large brown shopping bags.

I knew there would be some snow penetration when these items hit after I tossed them out of the plane to the climbers, but I felt that squashed fruit would fill the need as well as perfectly round specimens. The bombs weighed between five and six pounds each, bright netted bags easy to see and large tan shopping bags that I hoped would not get buried too deeply. We didn't have any parachutes for dropping cargo. Even if we had some, we probably wouldn't have used them because the winds would carry any parachute a long way off the intended drop zone. It would have to be a straightforward bombing run, with the idea to score hits on the ridge and not on the climbers!

DON WARNED ME to dress as if I were going to the North Pole. "It'll howl by your face at forty below, if not worse," he said, "and there is no way to heat the cabin with the door gone."

I knew I would face camera freeze-up and possible film breakage from the cold, so I loaded three Nikon cameras with motors and various lenses under my big Gerry down parka and kept a Tele-Rollei camera in an insulated camera box that was loaded with hand warmers. I would use the larger format if I had a superb picture lined up. Two cameras were loaded with Kodachrome 64 and two with Tri-X black-and-white film.

I wore hunter's mitts over a pair of silk mountaineer's finger gloves. If I had to make adjustments on the cameras, I could at least keep on the finger gloves. I tried to establish a basic exposure as we climbed up the side of McKinley in the droning turboprop.

Don said the winds aloft at that point were tricky and that I should dump three fruit bags off at every pass and take pictures as they fell and after they hit. He would have the plane flying slow enough, but the air would be bumpy.

The first drop missed the ridge by only ten feet, but it was ten feet of steep rocks that the climbers did not want to risk getting onto. The next drop was right on the group, and they had to dodge the missiles as they crashed into the snow around them. On the next pass, the canned juice fell ahead of their path, and they found only one of the three six-packs. I snapped a few frames through all these

airdrops. Then we flew back to make the kind of pix I really wanted: the climbers on the ridge and the peak behind.

I was working behind the plywood and not feeling the cold too much, more worried about the cameras freezing. Don had provided me with a long plastic tube that was connected to a main oxygen supply, and I was sucking on the tube in the high, thin air. Don also had a tube in his mouth, sucking in the oxygen.

I remember getting the Rollei out for the great black-and-white pix I had planned as the climbers were strung out on the ridge, waving. Someone held high a bag of grapefruit; probably Art Davidson or George Wichman. Ray Genet, with his bushy beard and short stature, was obvious.

I started to get woozy. I got the Tele-Rollei lined up

for one shot, made the exposure, and was cranking the film for another shot when I passed out.

DON WAS PAYING ATTENTION to the scene through his windshield and did not look back until after he made a climbing turn and heard the Rolleiflex rolling loudly across the deck. He saw me slumped over the plywood, half in and half out of the plane. A safety line was tied to my waist, but we found out later that it was longer than it should have been. If I had fallen out of the Beaver, I would have hung suspended from the modified doorway.

Don quickly banked the plane away from the ridge, and I rolled off the plywood divider and into the cabin. He said I looked like a red sack of potatoes. The oxygen tube was in my mouth, but my saliva had frozen in the tube and blocked the flow of the lifegiving gas.

The winds at 17,000 feet were picking up, and Don knew I could perish in a short time without the help of extra oxygen in that cold, thin air. He set the plane on a safe course and left the pilot's seat to go to me. He put his oxygen tube in my mouth and tried to revive me. Then he had to tend to the Beaver, which was bouncing around in very scary country. He was now without oxygen, so he whipped out his knife and cut a foot off the plugged oxygen tube that had been mine, and he started to draw the gas right away.

Trying to fly the big airplane in that windy place near the ridges below the summit would have tested his skill at any time. But on top of that, he had my unconscious body again rolling around the back of the plane with the tube pulled out of my mouth. He came back to me again and manhandled me to the seat, where he tied the safety rope to keep me stable and put the freshly cut oxygen tube in my mouth. He then turned up the flow of oxygen. It was this increased flow that saved me.

Don dove the plane for a lower altitude, and soon the thicker air below Kahiltna Glacier revived me. All I remember was seeing the five-hundred-dollar Tele-Rollei rolling around the back of the plane—and try as I might I couldn't reach it!

When I was alert enough, Don unwrapped the safety line and had me sit in the copilot's seat.

"You didn't say you wanted to be buried on Denali Pass," he said to me.

"What gave you that idea?" I asked.

"You were turning blue, the parka is red, and the white frost made you look very patriotic—like a burial at sea."

DON NEVER TOLD ME how he managed to get me from the back of the Beaver up to the seat, lash me down, and have me sucking on the oxygen tube, while still keeping an airplane that was new to him from "decorating Mount McKinley." I owe my life to him. And as for the expensive Tele-Rollei camera, it survived with just cosmetic damage and a dented sunshade.

It wasn't until well after the climb, when Art Davidson was recovering in the hospital from frostbite and exposure, that I learned how welcome our fruit drop had been. It was just what the thirsty men needed.

Not so pleasant was the anti-press feeling among most of the climbers, a sentiment directed at me along with everyone else who covered the big event. The climbers felt pressured by the press to produce results. Circling airplanes, photo attempts like ours, and jets zooming close enough to trigger avalanches made them even more anti-press.

But of course it was a press event. The first winter climb of Mount McKinley had to be. Ray Genet was in direct radio contact with a press office in Anchorage that provided him and the party with weather and other news. But with the exception of Art Davidson, none of the others wanted to be concerned with the press. They seemed to want to hold this world climbing event to themselves. There is not even one mention of our fruit-delivery flight in Davidson's book *Minus 148 Degrees*, the more-or-less official record of a cold and windy climb where many of the climbers suffered with frostbite and altitude sickness.

I didn't return to Talkeetna until the day the winter climbing party was being brought in. Instead of a normal fly-out from Kahiltna base, the epic climb turned into a military rescue involving two Huey helicopters and a circling C-130. Before the climbers could reflect on their experience, they were dumped into a huge welcoming party at Talkeetna airstrip—the very press event they wanted to avoid. And they had none of the answers the eager journalists demanded. They all reported it took weeks to get the solitude of McKinley out of their minds.

I'VE LINGERED ON STORIES focused on my friend Don Sheldon because in the course of covering Alaska and northwestern Canada for Time-Life News Service for more than seven years, I trusted my life to that man more than any other. I flew more air miles with him and thoroughly enjoyed every minute—well, almost every minute—of it. There were other old-timers with Don's skill. Bob Baker in Kotzebue was an excellent bush pilot, as was Pete Cesnun in Ketchikan and Bob Gruber in Homer. But Don had perhaps a wider variety of experience. He certainly put himself in harm's way at least as much as any pilot in

Alaska. He was a fine judge of weather and had a fairly photographic memory for places in his domain of central Alaska.

They say he wrecked forty-five planes, which may well be—but he never killed anyone in the process. The air was his natural element. When he walked on the ground, he sort of lumbered; he claims his knees were wrecked from hauling too much heavy game to the plane. But once in the air, he soared like an eagle.

Don Sheldon died in bed, to the amazement of every-one who knew his history of adventure in the air. He died of colon cancer in 1975. Don was the one man who never conformed to the saying that the cockpit is no place for an optimist. He was charged up with a positive spirit, even though his life every day between breakfast tea and late-night glass of milk was one of super-calculated risk. ✈

Chapter 13

The Two Lowells _____

Two of the most remarkable men I ever knew were named Lowell Thomas: the famous commentator, and his son, Lowell, Jr. My wife was the senior Lowell Thomas's secretary when he came to Alaska, about three months of the year. He personally sponsored me into the prestigious Explorers Club, and I will always be grateful.

Lowell, Jr., chose flying as a way of expressing himself and getting away from the pressures that bound his world-famous father to a microphone. He was an Army B-25 flier during World War II and a fine flight instructor. Lowell wanted the freedom of Alaska after completing his round-the-world flight with his wife, Tay, in their Cessna 180. He was good friends with Charles Lindbergh, and I am happy to say that I was able to meet and befriend Lindbergh when he came to Alaska just before I moved from the state in the early '70s.

Lowell fell in love with Alaska and wanted to make it his home, putting thousands of miles between himself and Hollywood, where he might have gravitated because of his desire to write and to produce pictures. Settling in Anchorage was perfect for him, and I spent many hours flying with him on my photo assignments as *Time-Life* magazine correspondent in Alaska for seven years.

I WENT OUT WITH LOWELL the first time after I had called him and asked if he would be available for some aerial photo work. I had an assignment at the time to shoot the offshore oil platforms in Cook Inlet for a petroleum industry magazine.

"What about right now?" he asked.

So we went up in his Cessna 180, the plane he brought to Alaska, and flew a dozen or so runs across the Cook Inlet ice pack to get pictures showing the giant oil platforms at work. One of the pictures, of a Marathon Oil platform with flaming gas flare, made the cover of the *New York Times* Sunday magazine two weeks later.

I was also working on another assignment for *Life*, covering the explosive eruptions of Mount Redoubt that were causing terrific mud slides and flooding and were dropping tons of debris on the surrounding area. I was having trouble finding a pilot who was prepared to put me near the erupting snow cone for a picture.

While Lowell and I were circling around the Cook Inlet oil platforms, using the snow-covered volcanoes and mountains of the Aleutian Range as a photo backdrop, he suggested we pop on over to see Mount Redoubt, which was fairly quiet that morning. At the mountain, Lowell's natural curiosity made him circle lower and lower over the caldera. Soon we were flying around inside the volcano, looking closely at the sulfur lake and the spouting gas. Luckily the big boy didn't belch while we were there. One burst and it would have been instant death from the super-hot blast and the poisonous gas.

LOWELL MADE THE MISTAKE of allowing a miner to bring pet huskies on board his plane for a flight to a new camp along the west edge of the Mount McKinley Park

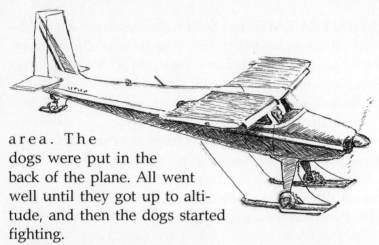

area. The
dogs were put in the
back of the plane. All went
well until they got up to altitude, and then the dogs started
fighting.

The dogs fought each other so hard and got the old
miner so involved in trying to calm them down that the
fracas took up the entire cockpit space. Lowell wondered
if he would be able to land the plane safely, or if the dogs
were going to do it another way. He managed to land, but
the cockpit was covered with dog blood and fur, and the
cabin headliner, side cloths, and seats were a mess.

When Lowell related this story to another bush pilot,
he immediately said that you never take two dogs in a
plane unless they are tied in gunny sacks! Or in cages in
the cargo space. There is something about high-altitude
flying or engine noise that drives dogs mad.

One lap dog that accompanied its master on a Mount
McKinley recon flight had much worse luck than the dogs
that got into a fight. The lap dog put up a fuss during the
flight, and the owner insisted all it needed was some fresh
air. If the pilot—it wasn't Lowell—would just crack the
window open, the dog could sniff the outside air as it did
when traveling with its owner in their mobile home. The
pilot complied. And the moment the window was opened,
the dog jumped out.

LOWELL THOMAS never wrinkled an airplane, as a civilian or a military pilot. He still has the Helio Courier he bought to cover Alaska years ago, and it's in good shape to pass on to his son.

Lowell used to be an owner of the air taxi business that Don Sheldon once ran. Lowell shared the operation with veteran mountain pilot Doug Geeting, but sold his share in 1989 to David and Julie Lee. Lowell began flying a new Cessna 207 powered by an Allison turbine for a powerful and quiet ride for his Mount McKinley recon passengers. He took up the premium McKinley sightseeing run for a select few people each season by flying out of both Camp Denali in the park and Talkeetna.

Before his retirement, Lowell's recon flight in his big, comfortable plane was perhaps the best way to see the splendors of the Alaska Range, but he was always booked through the season, and poor weather often pushed back his tight schedule. A flight with him up the Ruth Gorge and around Big Mac was hard to arrange, but if enough time was allotted or a party was willing to wait for a cancellation, it was more than worth it.

A number of outfits now offer McKinley flights out of Talkeetna. K-2, Talkeetna Air Taxi, Doug Geeting, and Cliff Hudson all do a good job. But to be flown by Lowell Thomas—the direct descendant of Don Sheldon—seemed to add to the thrill.

Lowell, at seventy-plus years, says he expects to die comfortably in bed years from now, having no known vices except for expensive cigars "once in a while."

THE BUSH PLANE AND PILOT will be on the Alaska scene for many more years, at least until the state is crisscrossed with freeways and streetcar lines. A report from

Anchorage indicates the pilots are as intrepid as always, delivering such items as a gas-powered outhouse to St. Lawrence Island for the comfort of one of the villagers and a tuxedo for some formally directed Aleut on St. Paul Island.

There was once a pizza rage in Southeastern Alaska, with one bush line shuttling hundreds of pizzas to the townspeople who had no other source—just a lucky pizza parlor a hundred air miles away. A bowling alley has been moved to someone's home by air, as have all sorts of animals. One bush airline, Reeve Aleutian Airways, which always offers the unexpected in service, brought a cow up to Nome so the kids could see where their milk came from. ✈

Chapter 14

Woman's Work _____

What about the first women flyers of Alaska? There were very few, although many of the old-time bush pilots taught their wives the elements of flying. When Charles Lindbergh came to Alaska in the summer of 1931, his wife, Anne, may have been the only woman pilot in Alaska at that time.

The Lindberghs took turns flying the Northrup-designed Lockheed Sirius floatplane, although Anne was officially listed as radio operator and navigator. Lindy was pioneering an air route along the so-called Great Circle Route to the Orient. Pan American, which subsidized the flight, hoped to arouse serious interest in a commercial route from the East Coast to the Orient via northern Canada and Alaska. The Lindberghs planned the trip so well that there were few times when they were in jeopardy. They landed behind schedule in Nome, but they had radioed ahead to report they would be late, knowing the world was watching every minute of the flight.

THE FIRST WOMAN taught and licensed to fly in Alaska was Mary M. Barrow, who was the wife of pioneering Canadian and Alaskan bush pilot Joe Barrow. She did what many wives have done when they want to learn to drive the family car: they hire someone to teach them when the husband is not around!

Before taking official flying lessons, Mary Barrow had been up dozens of times with Joe. She first met him when he was barnstorming around San Jacinto, California, a lovely little citrus fruit town across the mountain from Palm Springs. Joe took her flying, and she had no fear of the air. This was back in the mid-1920s, and with Joe's help, she soon toted up dozens of hours flying his plane— a two-wing fabric-and-stick frame assembly with a funny-looking engine and separate cockpits for pilot and passenger, a lot like a World War I fighter. After many years of following her husband's trade from California to Oregon, and into Washington, Canada, and Alaska, she became familiar with just about every popular plane that came on the market, but still she could not officially fly.

Her big opportunity came when her husband went to the East Coast to drum up interest in the idea of an Alaska airline. Mary Barrow checked into the only flying school around that offered her the chance to get lessons completed before her husband got back home, if she was lucky. She enrolled with Steve Mills at Merrill Field, Anchorage, and soon got a feel for flying the Fleet biplane he used for instruction. It was the only plane Mills owned, and any accident would wipe out that investment as well as her chance to get a flying ticket. She soloed on the 27th of July, 1932, on one of those days when the sky goes on forever. She spent $3.65 on a wire to Joe: "Soloed Safely This Morning!"

A few weeks later, the federal inspector tested the skills of twelve candidates at piloting the Fleet plane. She was the only woman to take the test, and one of only three candidates to pass. Official records indicate she was the first woman to take all her training and successfully pass the federal examination in Alaska. She always cherished that skill but seldom put it to practice. Much later, she took up residence near Beaverton, Oregon, and at the age of some ninety years, she was still able to recall the great times she had exploring Alaska in the early days of aviation.

ONE OF THE MOST FAMOUS and, for my money, nicest lady pilots was Ruth Hurst. Lady pilots are rare, lady pilots with commercial ratings are rarer, and lady pilots who operate their own air taxi service, as Ruth Hurst did, are an elite group, indeed. Take this train of thought and say that lady pilots who operate their own air taxi service and play the violin well enough to hold first chair in the Anchorage Symphony Orchestra are almost one of a kind. Ruth was one of a kind.

To keep vittles on the table, she flew a Cessna 180 on ski wheels in the winter and big wheels in the summer from Anchorage to a place almost no one ever heard of until the Iditarod Trail Sled Dog Race became popular: Skwentna. It was just a tiny village of twelve cabins scattered up and down the Skwentna River when I used to call there as a member of the Alaska State Police. If memory serves me, the state-graded airstrip was across the river from the village and its log-cabin post office run by old-time trapper Joe Delia.

Ruth served the village at least three days a week, flying in the mail and groceries and other supplies back in the '60s. When she had a full load of mail and other stuff, passengers often sat with boxes of groceries or other cargo in their laps, perhaps peeping out of the spotless windshield through a few stalks of celery. Ruth was very dependable but was also savvy enough to stay home in Anchorage when Cook Inlet's weather was sour. The trip to Skwentna usually took forty-five minutes, plus or minus the moose you saw along the way.

When there was a new addition to the symphony's repertory, she would bring her fiddle along and practice for a few minutes while waiting for Joe Delia to drag his canoe loaded with mail over the river ice from the post office. The lovely music of her violin would waft through the black spruce and across the snowy landscape. It was a merging of the best of two worlds.

WOMEN PILOTS WERE ALWAYS SUSPECTED of having failings that he-men of the north could poke fun at. A woman flier who asked someone else to check her engine oil one day came away from that request with the reputation of not wanting to get her hands dirty. Men talked about her dainty ways for many months after that incident.

I finally asked Ruth Hurst, who knew the woman in question, if there was any truth to the story. Ruth told me the woman had just been treated for a burned hand resulting from a kitchen fire. Wanting to keep the bandage clean, she asked a big-mouth pilot tied up next to her to help out. Ruth said the woman knew how to tear engines down and was never afraid of the tough work of being a pilot.

Both Ruth Hurst and Heidi Ruess of Anchorage can verify the feeling of being thought inadequate just because they were women taking on a so-called man's job. I've found women to be every bit as good as men in the air, only lacking when that last five-percent difference in body strength is needed for doing something like pushing a plane out of a mud hole.

Another woman pilot, Jo King, turned the tables on skeptics of her ability in the early '60s. Jo was an experienced pilot from the Lower 48 who began flying for Jimmix Samuelson's outfit in Bethel, on the lower Kuskokwim River, after getting her floatplane rating. She was just learning the Bethel region, no simple thing, when she was called to fly a passenger one morning to Hooper Bay, just off the Bering Sea. She had never been there, so she studied the charts carefully.

She got some tips on the flight from old-timer J. R. Havalson, a slightly built pilot of great experience. Some pilots said J. R. had spent so many hours flying Jimmix's Cessna floatplanes that his face had started to look like a reflection of the instrument panel. J. R. told Jo that she would be arriving in Hooper Bay at low tide, and he explained the landing and departure procedure in detail.

I've landed and taken off three times from Hooper Bay as a passenger in a floatplane, including both high and low tide. Flying into Hooper Bay is a lot like landing on an aircraft carrier. It takes a whole lot of nerve and, when the weather plays tricks, a whole lot of luck. J. R. told Jo that she would have to break all sorts of rules, doing things like taxiing on the mud for what seemed a mile and making high-torque turns to put her plane into a ready-for-departure mode. Jo gave him a big smile and headed for the floatplane dock, exuding all the confidence of an expert.

Jo's passenger dumped his groceries into the backseat of the plane and promptly went to sleep in the right-hand seat. He had not wasted his night in the Big City of Bethel by sleeping.

The flight to Hooper Bay was uneventful. She started her approach into the lagoon and brought the plane down onto the water, taxiing toward the village. Soon the water became thin enough to look like mud, but she kept the Cessna moving along until she had crossed a slough and spotted the muddy bank where some villagers had assembled. She revved up into a high-torque turn and, nice as could be, slid the tail end of the floats to the mud ramp and stopped the engine.

The passenger jumped out to take an end of the wooden plank the villagers had pushed out to the floats. Everyone helped unload the groceries and got to and from shore without wetting a shoe. Jo took a hike around the waterfront, which is far from imposing, and took a handful of mail from the teacher, who came down to meet her and was pleased to find a lady bush pilot. Without any other business to do, Jo climbed back into the Cessna and cranked up the engine, slid off the bank, and whipped the slough water into a froth. At high rev she taxied the plane across the mudflats, and once in the lagoon made her takeoff run into the bay.

The flight back to Bethel was without mishap. She

landed and taxied up to the floatplane dock, hoping someone would be there to take her mooring line, but there
was nary a hand to help. No problem. She made a grace-
ful leap to the dock and had the plane tied up in no time.

No one was at Samuelson's. She walked over to Leen's
Lodge, where she found half the Bethel flying corps waiting around a big table, sucking on coffee cups. At the other
end was J. R., waiting with a big smile and an outstretched
hand. Because of her quick round-trip flight, he knew that
she must have done everything right. Otherwise she
would still be out in the lagoon waiting for the tide to
change.

"How did it go at Hooper?" J. R. asked.

"Piece of cake, J. R. I landed in the lagoon, taxied across
the mudflats to the slough, found the mud ramp clear,
gave the bird a twist, and we were safe at Hooper. There
was no return business, so after I checked the village out,
I took her back out, and here I am for my coffee."

Handfuls of dollars descended upon J. R., more than
he could hold. Every pilot there had faced the horror of a
Hooper Bay landing, none had the advice of J. R. behind
them, and every one of them had bet she would founder
there.

"That's my girl!" J. R. yelled. "The dinner's on me
tonight!" ✈

Chapter 15

How Alaska
Got Its Wings

Alaska's first airplane—sort of—showed up in as unlikely a place as one could imagine: Nome, near the westernmost tip of the continent. A piano tuner named Henry Peterson became fascinated with the early reports of flying machines. With a long winter of dark days and nights ahead, he envisioned himself having ample time to build a machine that would carry him into the sky. He managed to secure plans from some outside source, much like one would order a plan to build a smoker out of an old fridge. He went to work building the plane from local materials. Alaskans have that feeling of invincibility. The fact that Peterson had never seen an airplane up close or talked to a pilot didn't deter him.

The year was 1911, and the Wright Brothers had flown the first powered aircraft more than seven years before. Everybody outside Alaska seemed to be flying one sort of crate or another—why not Henry Peterson?

He took over an unused mercantile warehouse and proceeded to put in long hours assembling the two-winged flier. Not much information came with the small engine that was included with the plans, so Peterson had to rely on the old trial-and-error system to figure things out. He didn't have any airplane wheels—but he didn't see an advantage to them over skis, anyway. So Peterson mounted his sky steed on some narrow hardwood strips that turned up properly at the ends.

As you might guess, the doors of the building where he constructed the plane couldn't open wide enough to allow the plane to be moved out. So helpers cut away the studded wall and pushed the contraption out into the snowy world.

On May 9, 1911, with all the tickets sold for this well-advertised Aviation Day, Peterson took his place in the rudimentary cockpit, turned the engine on, and waited for things to happen. Nothing did. Even friendly pushes and shoves would not break the inertia and turn the snowbird free. Sitting ahead of the pusher engine and between the fabric wings, Peterson soon realized the engine just did not have the power to move the plane and him down the snowy way to flight. He never tried to fly again.

TWO YEARS LATER, James Vernon Martin, an entrepreneur and a fine pilot for his day, brought a crated Gage-Martin biplane to Fairbanks on the steamer-river barge system and planned to put on a flying show. Martin had his flying certificate from the Royal Aero Club of England.

Martin and his wife sold tickets for a show on June 4, 1913, and plowed a suitable landing field in downtown Fairbanks. They were hoping that thousands would pay for a ten-minute ride, but only 250 signed up by the time the show went on. No one wanted to buy the plane when the show was over, so Martin crated it up and shipped it to Southern California. Fairbanks would later become an important hub of Alaskan aviation.

THE ARMY, trying out its new wings, was the next flying

visitor to the Territory. Taking off from Mitchell Field in Hempstead, Long Island, four De Havilland DH-4 biplanes began what became known as the Alaska Flying Expedition on July 20, 1920.

The Black Wolf Squadron's eight men soon received an education in northern cross-country flying as they dealt with bad weather, poor landing fields, and the immense task of flying across the continent to Nome.

A Lieutenant Kirkpatrick, flying No. 4 plane, made aviation history when he flew his biplane over the territorial capitol in Juneau on August 16, 1920. He couldn't land because there was no safe area to set down. But he dropped a parcel—the first "air express" delivery in Alaska—for Governor Thomas Riggs, Jr. Kirkpatrick then flew north to Whitehorse, in Canada's Yukon Territory, to reunite with the other planes.

The intrepid Army birdmen visited Dawson, Fairbanks, Ruby, and finally Nome. They landed at Fort Davis, three miles east of Nome, on August 23, 1920, where a veteran World War I combat pilot had laid out a landing strip on the old parade ground, creating the westernmost airfield in North America.

The Black Wolves made it back to Mitchell Field on October 20, 1920, after covering 8,690 miles in 110 flying hours.

ALASKA AND AVIATION were made for each other. Bush pilots—with usually a meager financial investment but with 200 percent of their energy and courage—soon became the binding sinew of the vast territory.

Dozens of books and articles have been written about early-day Alaska fliers, but no one tells the story better or with more understanding than retired Delta Airlines Capt.

Robert W. Stevens of Seattle. His remarkable *Alaskan Aviation History,* Volumes I and II, published in 1990, takes the reader from the days before aviation became a factor in Alaska to the rushing, gushing period of 1929-30 when many of the great names in bush and military flying made their mark.

For anyone addicted to aviation history, particularly of pre-statehood Alaska, these are the books to have. They're well-written and accurate, with outstanding photographs and illustrations. Captain Bob has spent a lifetime collecting the facts and pictures for this wonderful work of love that offers solid information along with those delectable tidbits that make history come to life for both researcher and casual reader. These first two volumes are the most sought-after flying books in the Alaska library system.

THE REAL GROWTH IN BUSH AVIATION came during the '30s and '40s, when everyone with enough cash to buy a crate and get it above Ketchikan had notions of serving the scattered public on a paying basis.

It was big business for bush pilots to make arrangements with mine operators to get their people back to Anchorage or Fairbanks before the bad weather locked them in at the mine site. Oscar Winchell, who operated Star Airlines from Anchorage, flew into the mine located between McGrath and Ruby with his Pilgrim, a two-winged passenger plane that offered six places in the cabin. The pilot sat in his own fresh-air cockpit above the wings and had great visibility but no way of checking on the passengers.

Winchell brought the big bird into the mining strip that, even under the best of conditions, was known to pose

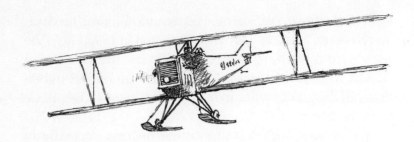

a calculated risk for both landing and takeoff. But he had the hazards of a short and bumpy runway coupled with high trees on the downhill end all worked out in his mind. Bush pilots made their living on conquering risk.

Winchell landed one time and was surprised to see twice the number of men ready to go out for the winter, and all of them with big personal kits to go, too. He told the gang that he would have to make two trips, and he pushed the first six fellows into the cabin and got them seated and buckled in. He then walked around the plane and climbed up to his cockpit.

The other miners didn't want to take a chance of being stranded there for the winter. With Winchell out of sight as he got into the isolated cockpit, the other miners tossed their gear into the cabin and jumped on top of the pile.

Winchell, caught up in his cockpit checklist and other duties, took his time revving up. He let the brakes off and opened up the throttle until the Pilgrim was rolling along. But the tail wouldn't lift and, even worse, the plane refused to fly as it rolled toward the forest edge.

The crash into the trees scraped off the plane's undercarriage and caused some other damage, but no one was hurt. Winchell came down from his cockpit and got the passengers out of the cabin. He was shocked to see the jumble of people and gear that tumbled out.

He said out loud to no one in particular: "It would have been a helluva paying trip if we had made it!"

THE COLD WAR between the United States and the Soviet Union brought some unexpected chances for offbeat aviation incidents. Take polar bear hunting, for example. For some reason, just about all the polar bears taken by U.S. trophy hunters were being bagged on the Soviet side of the International Date Line, the imaginary line that separates tomorrow from today and that runs between Big and Little Diomede islands in the Bering Strait between Alaska and Russia.

Flying polar bear hunters into Russian territory was illegal. The U.S. government frowned on it but had no effective way to patrol the region without further exciting the Russians and perhaps creating an incident. During the late '50s and '60s, the sparks would fly between the two giant powers for almost any reason.

To make the polar bear hunt more interesting, pilots would take their clients along the Chukchi Sea coast of Siberia. One day in Nome, I had a visit from some happy polar bear hunters who had asked their pilot to drop them off in Nome so they could see the town. The hunters were sitting in the bar showing off Polaroid prints of them visiting Siberian Eskimo villages. One had even taken a picture of their second plane buzzing a giant Soviet radar antenna.

While this may sound like a typical Joe College stunt, the Soviets took this kind of thing very seriously and would put fighters up over the Bering Strait. This would trigger our DEW Line radars and wake up some sleepy general on Pentagon standby duty, and we would send our F-102s up from their Alaskan bases. Since the bear-hunting planes could scoot home over the ice at a very low altitude, avoiding radar, the fighters from both sides would mill around over the Chukchi Sea, waiting for the order to shoot. World War III was a dumb trick away.

One Air Force intelligence officer told me the Soviets were not so worried about direct attack, but rather that the visits to their coastal villages would become a tourist attraction and eventually U.S. spies would gain concealed entry into the Siberian region.

During the Cold War, scrambles over the frozen wastelands of the arctic were not uncommon. The orders were that no shots or missiles could be fired unless certain conditions were met. This, of course, didn't satisfy the hot-blooded fighter jocks who cavorted about the polar sky. At least once, and perhaps twice, a U.S. dogfight with a Soviet MiG fighter resulted in a wild display of aerobatics between pilots who knew they could not use their guns or missiles.

The Russians one day flew a Bear bomber right down the main street of Nome, about 500 feet off the deck. The huge plane buzzed in and buzzed out and was never caught. ✈

Chapter 16

The Family Way _____

Alaska is unique in the United States in that it demands the use of air travel to gain access to both its interior and fringes from the few ports and railheads. When I arrived in Alaska at statehood in 1959, one in every seventeen residents owned an airplane. One in five was a licensed pilot. Today the ratio is much different, reflecting the improvement in all forms of transportation, and a far lower percentage of citizens own or fly planes.

Once our family settled in Anchorage after a few months in Cordova, we soon saw the advantage of aircraft ownership. Without any licensed pilots in the family, but with a strong yen to see the state, we found a group of pilots that needed a fourth investor in taking over a Cessna 180 floatplane. We joined them for $7,500—and discovered that owning an aircraft is very much like owning a boat. They used to say that a sailboat or sportfishing boat was a wooden hole in the water through which you throw money.

Everything in, on, or for an airplane costs at least three times more than for a seagoing or land-traveling craft. Airplane parts are special items with special numbers on them. These parts are often installed by specially trained and certified mechanics, and the parts must be inspected by these same expensive people—after every few hours of flying time!

You can run your old Jeep with hardly a care as to when the starter belt was last replaced or the spark plugs were checked. But you don't dare move your plane from its appointed parking space today without full clearance and certification by the "guvmint"—or face a fine and a blemish on your otherwise clean flying record.

But despite all the rules, Alaskans have a way of doing things their own way. For instance, flying without a license. It's done all the time in the Bush and often on long cross-country flights. My son David found that out one summer during vacation from high school, when he worked at a placer gold mine near Bluff, Alaska, not far from Nome. He learned to repair diesel front-end loaders and overhaul the engine of a middle-aged Taylor Cub aircraft, and he learned all about girls. An Eskimo village was near the mine, and the teenagers played together. The older ones taught the younger ones the secrets of Marlboro cigarettes, Olympia beer, and the birds and bees.

When winter weather ended mining for the year, the owner took David back to Fairbanks, where we were then living, allowing him to fly the T-craft most of the way. After a few days of filling up on home cooking, David took off with the T-craft owner for a flight to San Carlos, California, via Seattle. They made it in a week or so, with just a few alarums and excursions to keep the flight from being boring. David again flew most of the way.

I was happy for David to have his chance to fly, and I looked forward to having a pilot in the family to support my aerial photography needs. My friends told me I'd be lucky not to kill myself if I insisted on doing the low-level flying myself. For David's high school graduation present,

I planned to pay for his training to get a private pilot's license and for forty hours of flying. To my surprise, he turned me down when I suggested it. The tab would have been around fifteen hundred dollars—but the boy chose a shiny brass trumpet for five hundred dollars instead.

I also gave my other son, Steven, a chance to get a private pilot's license—and he declined, too, and chose something he wanted more. Both boys followed a path into the University of Alaska and careers involving forms of photography. My older son, David, became a principal force at the leading ad agency in Anchorage and has many creative talent awards to his credit—walls of them. Steven chose both music (he has a rock band) and film. He became one of the finest 16mm and video cameraman in Alaska, owning his own production company—Moving Picture Company of Anchorage—and shooting projects all over the world.

Flying bored my boys, and even today when they take the controls of a chartered plane just for fun, their eyes still leave the instrument panel and the horizon ahead to seek out the wonderful photo subjects below—my problem for years!

I LEARNED SOME HANDS-ON FLYING MYSELF, thanks to Gene Farland, a veteran Air Corps B-17 pilot and longtime Alaska bush pilot. He taught me enough to get off the ground and fly around what was once Marks Army Air Field at Nome.

I felt pretty good soloing the Taylorcraft on cold, high-pressure winter afternoons. Gene told me that because of the thick air during periods of high pressure, it was hard not to fly the plane safely. He showed me how he let the T-craft fly itself, banking the plane with his body weight alone. The little yellow bird was reluctant to land, the flying was so easy.

"The air is too thick to crash," Farland said, as he demonstrated a return to even flying as soon as power was applied.

The closest I came to death at Nome's aerodrome was a time when Farland taxied to the far end of the longest runway and waited for clearance. The Taylorcraft could have taken off from the flight line or taxiway because it was so light, but Farland was teaching me proper procedure.

After a few minutes, a lumbering C-123 Fairchild cargo carrier of the Alaska Air National Guard showed up. Rather than let us get off and on our way, the C-123 pilot insisted he had right-of-way. He kept revving his engines and making adjustments.

After a few more minutes of this delay, Farland asked for permission to take off. The Air Guard pilot got up on his rights and demanded that we wait for him. He said he was a senior pilot and spouted a lot of other BS.

Farland got on the radio to the tower.

"Tell Colonel Hotshot that I was flying B-17s over Schweinfurt while he was still wetting his rompers, and if he can't figure out how to make it go up, we are leaving!"

And we started our roll just as the C-123 rolled toward us.

Farland was as mad as I've seen him. He held the T-craft on the deck until just the right moment and then let it leap into the air and to the left as the big silver bird roared by. There were screams for aircraft numbers and claims that reports would be filed, but in the end nothing was done.

As we moved on down the frozen coastline toward

Bluff, Farland made some comment about how he hoped the pilot had brought along some spare underwear.

THE KIND OF FLYING that makes for interesting conversation after the event is often referred to as "white-knuckle" by the participants. Even the pilot! This kind of "interesting" travel happens not only under the hands of bush pilots, that dying breed, but of certified air transport pilots who would be red-faced if you called their work "air taxi" flying, the legal term for much of the Far North's short-hop aviation.

Today there are pilots based almost everywhere, ready to take you most anyplace for a price, and if you are lucky and they're having a good day, they will bring you back with some memorable "interesting" moments.

Glenda, the woman who cooks my breakfast from time to time and handles the checkbook all the time, was not too interested in flying. We met and were married after I left Alaska in the early '70s. She told me—a guy as accustomed to bush planes as automobiles—that she would never think of getting into anything with less than four "motors," as she refers to engines.

She was first airlifted in the early days of the Boeing 707 passenger jet and never considered any plane with less power to be truly reliable. But then some great planes appeared under the Douglas, Lockheed, Boeing, and other labels that had only two "motors." She told me she didn't want to know about them. She would get on one, order a double Scotch as soon as possible, and knead her hands until the contraption was safely back on the ground.

So with this attitude, I figured it was going to be a disappointing vacation for me, returning to my home in Alaska in 1985 but knowing I would not be able to share a

Cessna floatplane ride with her to a great rainbow fishing hole. She started making anti-one-motor noises even in Seattle when a small plane landed as our Alaska Airlines silver giant waited for takeoff.

Glenda would be the stay-behind while I and another couple toured the treetops in a friend's Cessna 185 on floats, seeking proper rainbow trout fishing. But when the day came and I started to gear up, she began putting on boots and fishing vest as well. Very thoughtful of her, I thought, seeing us off in costume. But lo and behold, she was the first person boarded by the pilot, who put her up front where the action was. She was going to give it a try.

We fisher-types settled onto the rear bench and seats. The departure was as lovely as one could imagine: the engine roaring, the water spraying picturesquely from the plane's path as the Cessna sought the thinner air and drippingly departed from the water.

Perhaps there is something comforting about looking down and seeing the plane's sturdy Edo float. In any case, Glenda was soon pointing out other float planes in the sky and, looking down, said she saw her first moose. From that day forward, my only problem was keeping her out of hundred-and-fifty-dollar-an-hour floatplanes.

The pilot confessed to me later that Glenda didn't really see a moose. He had flown over a commercial musk ox farm near Talkeetna, and she had seen one of those hairy arctic creatures foraging amid the black spruce. He said moose would come later, an easy transition. ✈

Chapter 17

Is Alaska Great, or What!

Our home in Anchorage was the crossroads of the world for hundreds of people I knew professionally and as friends, or as friends of friends. They would call from Anchorage International after a flight from Tokyo, with perhaps a seven-hour layover before a connecting flight back East. We often managed to turn that dead time for them into an exciting look at Alaska.

I recall one of my New York editors from *Time* calling me from the airport early one June morning in the late '60s. He just wanted to say hi, but I was only ten minutes from the airport, so I soon had him home with us for a breakfast of homemade cinnamon rolls and coffee. He just wanted to see Anchorage. But I learned that he was an ardent trout fisherman, accustomed to casting to mirror-like pools in the Pennsylvania spring creeks. Brook trout and an occasional brown were his big thrill.

In no time I had him outfitted with my wife's spare hip boots, a fishing vest, and my Fenwick fiberglass fly rod with a weight-forward No. 5 Sunset line on it. The rod was rugged, and it took a lot of punishment from borrowing friends and always managed to deliver a full load of fish, as long as the operator could keep the line in the water.

On that day, it happened that some of the ladies who shared our Cessna 180 floatplane decided to cross Cook Inlet to Alexander Creek to catch some salmon for a church barbecue that night. There was room in the back for my New York friend and his leather wallet full of dynamite fishing flies. He tucked his old Leica II camera into a plastic sandwich bag, and I had the group of them down to the plane on Lake Hood in a short time. We stopped briefly at the bait shop on Spenard Road for a visitor's license for my Eastern fly fisherman. I'd put that on my next *Time* expense account under "research materials."

They roared off into the clear morning sky, leaving a lovely rooster tail hanging in the air over the lake. I went back to being a correspondent until later in the day when I was alerted to their return by a call from the FAA tower, saying the plane would be landing in ten minutes. By the time the plane arrived, I was waiting with the VW bus, my big Styrofoam cooler yawning empty, ready for a load of fresh fish. I hoped someone had caught something, just to maintain Alaska's reputation as a great place to fish.

The Cessna bounced in and made a power turn into the shore. There seemed to be some anxiety about getting tied up. The ladies hopped out, all smiles, followed by my New York friend. He was almost speechless. The flight! The fishing! The wilderness so near Anchorage! (About twenty-five minutes away.)He wanted to spill it all out, but I told him to save it for lunch.

THEY HAD HIT IT BIG at Alexander Creek. The tide was right or the casting was good or Alaska was just living up to its reputation. Each person had three salmon, which made twelve nice silvers. And there were another twelve in the floats—above the legal limit! Feeling a little stupid about this fishing violation being thrust into my hands but not wanting to waste fish that would be prime fare for the church barbecue, I put the fish from the floats into a burlap bag. Then I put the legal catch in the cooler box for the ride home.

We cleaned the salmon in the backyard, with the garden hose flicking off the loose scales and the insides. My friend was amazed at how quickly the job went. The dog, Countess Dagmar, tried to play brown bear and take a fresh silver for herself. No way!

After the yard was cleaned up, my friend told me about the fishing. He said the fish attacked his offering on every single cast—even his first roll cast, when his wooly-worm fly hit the water with an unprofessional plop. He was overjoyed. Never had fishing like it—and no fish under six pounds! After his first three catches, he spent his time taking snapshots of the ladies with their Mitchell 300 spinning outfits making strike after strike with No. 3 Mepps and Daredevils.

One of them suggested he walk back to a small creek nearby and try his luck there—just for fun. He found the bank willows too close for any sort of fly casting at the creek, so he rolled out the smallest of the wooly worms. Wham! A large rainbow trout swallowed it up. He realized he had to fight and land the fish without a net or help from the ladies who had beached his silvers.

He was out into the creek mouth and soon over his depth, but he kept the rainbow on a taut line and soon horsed the tired fish to shore. He put it on the stringer and lashed that around a snag. With the next cast, the black fly never even hit the water before a big rainbow had it and was off for the bottom. He soon added that to the stringer and was pulling line free from the old Medalist

reel to cast again when the ladies called time. He was dragging the well-chewed fly through the boot-deep water, starting to walk back to the Cessna, when another rainbow took the line and ran.

I asked where the rainbows were. He admitted he had tucked them into the back of the vest and forgotten to mention them. I found the loaded vest in the VW and cleaned the fish.

"I guess we'll have these for lunch, if you don't mind," I said. "We're tired of salmon."

After lunch he took a nap, filled with fresh rainbow fried in butter and covered in slivered almonds, my favorite style. While he slept, I slipped off to the locker plant at Tenth and M, where I had the three largest salmon flash-frozen and packed for flight in a "suitcase pack" that could be shipped as baggage with no chance of defrosting.

Later we toured Anchorage, met a few of my more colorful friends, and then packed up for my friend's continuing trip home to New York. I knew the counter people at Northwest Airlines, so I got him a no-smoking window seat and told the clerk he would be there about ten minutes before boarding—not to worry. A skycap took all the baggage including the frozen pack, and my friend was on his way home a few minutes later, an *Alaska Sportsman* magazine to support his dreams.

I received a call at home at 3 A.M., and by the time I got my head clear, my friend was into his second paragraph of thank yous. He was very surprised to find the pack of perfectly frozen silver salmon—the big three. I told him to tell his wife and dinner friends that they should have seen the ones that got away! ✈

Chapter 18

Strip Mining ⎯⎯⎯⎯⎯⎯⎯⎯⎯⎯

My wife's friend Lucy came through Alaska on a tour that dumped her in Anchorage with ten days free until her plane returned to Seattle.

Of course we took Lucy in, and after a fine moose dinner tried to make some sense out of all the things she wanted to see while she was "up North."

There was Mount McKinley, grizzly bears eating salmon, polar bears chasing seals, Eskimos dancing and blanket-tossing, and a typical Native village above the Arctic Circle—one with a cheap gift shop. She thought she'd maybe try some easy fishing. And she wanted to meet some of the Alaskan characters we had told her about. She had just shed a husband, and she thought an Alaskan, complete with whiskers and a gold mine, would be just what she needed.

So I suggested we drive up to Talkeetna for (1) the characters, (2) a chance at seeing McKinley on a recon flight with Don Sheldon, and (3) easy fishing; the salmon were pouring up the Susitna River into the Talkeetna and Chulitna. Can't miss!

We introduced Lucy to Evil Alice Powell, owner and grand factotum of the Talkeetna Motel. Alice took Lucy on a fern-picking hike the first day, and we had fiddlehead ferns with Sauce Alicia that night, with fresh-caught salmon steaks.

The next morning, after filling our bellies with blueberry sourdough hotcakes and French-roast coffee, we walked through the back roads to Don Sheldon's home. The flight strip next to his house is complete with five or six single-engine planes, a gas pump, and a seldom-used hangar. He normally caters to the mountaineers wanting to add McKinley to their list of "have climbed." Don was out on a flight, but mountain guide Ray Genet was there, trying to find out from Don's wife, Roberta, when the flier would be ready to move another party up to base camp on the Kahiltna Glacier.

Ray and Lucy hit it off right away. "The Pirate" never let a good-looking woman get by him. He was known for flying voluptuous females up onto the glacier, where he would persuade them to pose in the buff, saying he was shooting for *Playboy* magazine. Ray kept a flow of Ektachrome nudity headed toward Chicago and Hugh Hefner's editors. Later on, *Playboy* did send an official centerfold photographer to Alaska.

Lucy wasn't interested in going anywhere with Ray, however. We had found a pilot who might be able to take her into the Range. I told her that when the pilot felt the weather was just right and he could assure her of a beautiful flight to McKinley and back via the Ruth and Kahiltna glaciers, he would give her thirty minutes notice. In the meantime, I told Lucy, Talkeetna is a delightful place to wander around in. Its 250 people live at some ease in log cabins or simple frame homes set in the hardwood forest that fills the banks between the Talkeetna and Susitna rivers. I told Lucy to wander around and meet the folks.

But Lucy was antsy to get going. The pilot's wife then

told Lucy that if she just wanted to fly into a mining camp and come right back, her husband could take her on a flight to deliver medicine and groceries to Cache Creek.

"YEAH! LET'S GO!" Lucy said. She got in the back seat of the tiny yellow Piper Cub, a box of prescriptions on her lap, her knees up against the pilot's seat. She squealed with delight as the plane bounced down the dirt strip in "downtown Talkeetna" and leaped into the air. The Cache Creek mine of the Brendels was just a few minutes away by air, though it's many hours overland by sleds and a tractor in the winter when heavy supplies are moved into camp.

We amused ourselves sipping Oly at the Roadhouse Hotel, where the burly bartender was holding forth with a series of stories about some of the Talkeetna characters. We had exchanged some stories and got a laugh out of each by the time the yellow Cub came in over the strip and bounced down, turned around down by the river, and taxied back to the gas pumps. The pilot popped out. Then a woman—not Lucy—emerged from the back seat, a big towel wrapped around he face. I asked what happened to Lucy.

"Well, we made it in to the strip at the mine, but the medicine was just too late," the pilot said. "It looks like Emmy here has an abscessed tooth. I had to leave Lucy there."

So there was Lucy, stuck at the Cache Creek mine while the pilot took care of getting Emmy Brendel to a dentist. Emmy climbed into the Cub after he made a phone call, and off they flew for the town of Willow to find the dentist. By the time the plane returned again, it was pitch dark.

"I was wondering what plans you got for Lucy," I said.

He explained that, for the time being, he had no plans whatsoever for Lucy. She would have to wait at the mine.

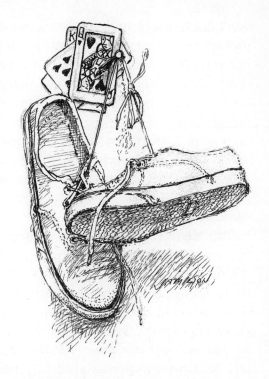

"I got a crack-of-dawn load to go up to base camp on the mountain, weather permitting," he explained, "and I should follow that with the rest of the party supplies or else they are going to stand around waiting for hours." Lucy was last in line for his services.

I could see he was tired and there was nothing else to do. I only hoped that Lucy was having a fair time with all those horny-handed miners, she in her skintight jeans and cute tennis shoes.

We got the whole story the next day after Mike Fisher and I had destroyed a mountain of Alice's blueberry hotcakes with real maple syrup, and some homemade caribou sausages on the side, washed down with a quart of milk.

We heard the sputter of the Piper engine, cranking down for the landing. We jumped in Mike's pickup and went out to the strip. Lucy was aboard the plane. The pilot had picked up Emmy Brendel that morning, dropped her off at the mining camp with some groceries and a chocolate cream pie that she had juggled on her lap, and brought Lucy out before the miners could chase her from the camp.

It seems the miners needed something to keep themselves busy after Lucy cooked up a dinner of creamed salmon chunks on sourdough bread toast. Someone suggested a little poker, just to kill the time until the plane came back. Lucy admitted she had never played the game before, staying pretty much to bridge and 500 rummy—but she was agreeable to being taught if the twenty-dollar bill she kept crammed in her pocket purse would get her in the game. The men were gracious enough to lead her through the intricacies of five-card stud, low ball, hi-low Jacks, and other varieties of the game.

"Look," she told me. "I still have my twenty-dollar bill! And two hundred and fifty dollars more!"

She had cleaned out the miners' ready cash and then refused to play strip poker or to accept IOUs, claiming she wouldn't be in "town" long enough to wait for their payday. She then asked one of the miners to trade some cash for one of the fancy nuggets all the men had stashed in tobacco tins and olive bottles. She wanted to have a pendant made to remind her of the evening at Cache Creek Mine. She paid for the nugget with all the fives and tens she had—and it struck the fellows like lightning that they now had enough cash to begin the game again.

By the time the yellow bird landed, she had that hundred back. But as a consolation prize, she left her tennis shoes for the men to nail to the bunkhouse wall. They wanted to be able to claim that they had played strip poker with her and that the shoes were the last bit of clothing that went on the table. She told me that's the way all these wild Alaska stories get going—just an evening of "funnin'." ✈

Chapter 19

The Two Alices _____

While Lucy was off on her adventure at the Cache Creek mine, and we were passing the time at the Roadhouse Hotel, we heard the bartender's tale of the wildest scene Talkeetna had witnessed during World War II. It had to do with Cantwell Alice (not to be confused with Evil Alice Powell), the fabled boss of the all-girl section gang on the Alaska Railroad that runs through Talkeetna. The railroad was short of male workers during the war. Cantwell Alice was one strong lady, and she ran the ten gals under her with an iron hand because she wanted "no crap" from the roadmaster about how they were doing compared with the male work gangs.

As the bartender told it, the incident began one cold night as smoke was curling comfortably up from the coal stoves in the sleeping cars occupied by the women's section gang. A little after eleven, there was a commotion in one of the cars. A man from the village had decided that on such a cold night, the ladies could use some company. He had prepared for his night away from home by taking off his boots, outer clothes, and everything but his long johns. He crept down to the end of the car, where Cantwell Alice had the corner to herself, and crawled into bed with her.

It wasn't but a second or so before the car exploded in screams and yells, and bodies were flying around in the dark. A human form was tossed from the open door of the car into the snow, and it was followed by Cantwell Alice in her nightgown, kneeboots unlaced, running like hell after the fleeing form that was dressed only in long johns. Cantwell Alice kept trying to get a bead on the body ahead with a lever-action .30-30 rifle that was kept in the camp car to scare off bears. After five shots with no blood drawn, she allowed the flying long johns to take the lead into the dark night.

No one ever knew who the horny nightwalker was, but since everyone in the village was awakened by the shooting, there were several ideal suspects the next day. Cantwell Alice made it known that next time, she would start shooting sooner and have a trophy to show all the gals in her crew.

I ALMOST MET CANTWELL ALICE, in a way. We didn't actually sit down and exchange railroading stories over a beer, but I did watch her in action, years after the long-johns incident, when she dropped in to see her old pal Alice Powell at the Talkeetna Motel. Alice Powell seldom had time to sit around with a drink in front of her, but she did set up a house Oly for Cantwell Alice and then ran off, after a few sips of ginger ale, to make some adjustments to the oven where several pies were baking.

I was off in a corner by the spiral stairs, using what daylight came in through the half-open front door in trying to untangle the line on a Penn fishing reel. Cantwell Alice was sitting there nursing her beer when one of the miners from the Peters Creek mining district came in and looked around in the dim light. He was in bib overalls,

and his knees were a bit wet from grubbing around with some machine back at the mine. He must have just been dumped off from a bush flight to get some groceries and see the bright lights of Talkeetna.

Of course the miner noticed Cantwell Alice sitting there, sipping the last bubbles from her brown bottle. When Alice Powell rounded the bend from the kitchen and saw him, he asked for an Oly.

"And get one for the lady, too—on me," he said. "Put it on my tab, Ms. Powell."

The miner was always a bit formal when making his first credit request of the day. He would revert to "Alice" later on.

Alice Powell delivered the bottled goods, and Cantwell Alice wasted no time in taking a big swig and then burping. She never looked at the expectant miner, just went on drinking. He sipped his beer real fast and had Alice set up another one for both of them, hoping to force Cantwell to acknowledge his gift. Nothing.

Alice Powell flitted back and forth, preparing for the

dinner hour. She always had half a dozen fresh salmon to feed the guests—fish they had caught and wanted to eat right away. For the villagers and for drop-in customers like the miner, she kept a pile of thawed T-bones, an inch thick, ready to hit the charcoal grill. It was the best-spent seven-fifty in Alaska as it included a complimentary glass of house red and some crispy hard rolls that were said to be made from the first sourdough starter to cross the Klondike.

In an hour there were seven empties in front of Cantwell Alice, and the miner was starting to get a little worried about his ten-dollar investment in friendship. When Alice Powell delivered the next bottles, the miner took his and moved on down the bar to a stool next to Cantwell Alice.

"If you don't like Oly we can order sumpin' else," he said. There was no response from the woman.

He finished his beer and was about to call for another when he screwed up his face into a smile and poked his head in front of Cantwell Alice and said, "You know, I spent a day's diggins on you and you don't even say boo— I think I'm cuttin' you off!"

Cantwell Alice picked up her last bottle, which had an inch or so of beer in the bottom, and tipped it into her mouth, then turned to face the miner. She crushed the Oly bottle in her right hand, dropping the mess in front of him, and said, "You know, you talk too fuckin' much," and walked out. ✦

Chapter 20

The Unfriendly Skies ———

Bill Munz wasn't the only bush pilot I'd just as soon not fly with. I remember the time as a state policeman that I had to escort an IRS intelligence agent, the only one in Alaska then, to a remote mine because he felt uncomfortable going alone. We sat at a corner table at Alice Powell's restaurant in Talkeetna one frosty morning, having breakfast after driving the 125 miles up from Anchorage.

Sitting at another table was a fellow, all bundled up, having only coffee. He was pouring some clear liquid from another cup into the coffee, apparently to cool the coffee down. He finished two cups and then told us he was heading out to the village airstrip and would have the plane ready when we got there. He was our pilot. I would never have taken him for a pilot, as he had none of that look. He looked more like a bum just off a drunk.

We finished our breakfast, and Alice packed us two sandwiches and two canned Cokes in a brown bag. She asked where we were going. The IRS man gave me the evil eye, so I didn't say anything. He told Alice we were flying with the man who had breakfast just ahead of us.

"Well, when I don't see you fellows tonight, I'll have some idea where to send the others to look for you," she said. "We know the color of his plane."

I wasn't sure what she meant. But I didn't think anything of it, other than it might be a dangerous mission the agent was on. It turned out to be an easy audit, however. The miner, who was almost dormant with arthritis, had little income to show and had kept meticulous records. It seems that one of his jealous friends "turned him in."

When we got back to Talkeetna, I asked Alice what she meant by her remarks before we left.

"You know that so-called bush pilot you went with," she said. "He drinks a lot and I never know when he's going to screw himself into the ground out there. He had two cups of coffee and two cups of vodka this morning, and that was his breakfast!"

ART JOHNSON, who flew a bush route for Wien Alaska Airways, was my first choice whenever I could get out of flying with Munz Northern. The problem with fine outfits like Wien was that they had so much business, they had little time to fool around with police work, like waiting while I combed a village for a low-grade crook or allowing us to fill their plane with prisoners and witnesses to the detriment of their regular customers.

Art told me that my dollar was as good as anyone's. But he liked to remind me that the police could not expect special service from bush pilots, such as guarding a prisoner in the backseat, when that same fellow would likely be a free villager the next week and seeking a flight somewhere. The prisoners had long memories about how they flew to the Nome jail.

Art was killed during a bad whiteout over Safety Lagoon, just southeast of Nome, when he drove his Cessna into the ice nose-first from 3,000 feet while talking to Nome FAA about where he was. The FAA people heard the engine wind up on the dive—and then nothing. He had been returning from an emergency medical flight.

I was the first one on the scene three days later when the weather allowed us to see a few feet ahead of our tracked vehicles. The Cessna was wrinkled up from nose to behind the wing like an accordion. We had to pry the doors off. Inside we found the emergency victim that Art had flown to help. She was a woman who had fallen off a stool in her kitchen and hit her head on the table. She was now dead, and frozen solid. Art Johnson was dead. Both seat belts held, but the seats didn't. They were rammed into the front cabin floor space. Behind the seats was a bundle of Christmas trees, with my name on one of them.

I later checked on the dead woman and learned that she had been drinking before the accident. The medics in Kotzebue confessed that she probably was not hurt as badly as everyone first thought when the emergency radio call came in. Village first-aiders sometimes like to pump up a medical case just to get on the radio and play a role. Later, investigators determined that propeller failure was the cause of the crash.

I recall one reported emergency in which the first-aider at one village called the medic in Kotzebue to report a child who had pronounced red-and-green spots on her face and neck. None of the medical references helped in diagnosis, but the symptoms came close to those of a spotted fever common to the Congo River drainage. The girl had to be flown to Kotzebue, and a bush pilot named Bob Baker was hired for the job. In Kotzebue, the medics discovered that the girl, more scared than sick, had been using poster paints in school. The kids had started to spray each other by flicking the brushes. The cure was Ivory soap and hot water.

THE FIRST ATTEMPTED SKYJACKING in Alaska occurred on a Munz Northern Airways plane, long after Bill Munz was gone and Dick Gallagher had taken over the operation. The culprits in the case turned out to be a couple of Bureau of Indian Affairs carpenters.

The carpenters had arrived in Nome with orders to proceed to Gambell, on St. Lawrence Island, to make repairs to the government school during the summer vacation in 1962. I knew the teachers there very well, because I flew on patrol to Gambell at least once a month during summer and every three months in winter.

Gambell airstrip was socked in when the carpenters arrived in Nome from Anchorage. Rather than taking a hotel room and resting while they waited for the weather to clear, they decided to spend their time in the Breakers Bar on Main Street. The Munz agent knew they were in the bar, and they were still there three hours later when the weather cleared for their flight. The pilot had the men picked up at the bar and delivered to the speedy twin-engine Aero Commander.

After takeoff the copilot saw the men sipping beer from cans they had stored in their flight bags. He told them the airline had no license to serve intoxicants and said it was illegal for them to drink in the plane on their own. They put the cans away but soon began drinking again. The copilot again ordered them to stop.

The carpenters made some half-threatening remarks. And when they were told to buckle up for landing at Gambell, they demanded to be taken to Hawaii (something like three thousand miles to the south) or to Siberia (only a short distance to the west) so they could get a drink. The pilot and copilot ignored them and set the plane down, happy to see the men get off.

So it was a big surprise when the men again demanded that the plane take them to Hawaii. A pipe wrench or crowbar was swung, and soon a wild fight was under way between the pilots and the carpenters. One pilot tried to fight the carpenters off as the other got into the cockpit to start the engines for a getaway. The prop wash knocked the carpenters off balance. As the plane began to move with one engine firing and the other one starting up, the pilot on the ground jumped in and slammed the door against the attackers.

BACK IN NOME, I was sorting the mail and shuffling reports when the call came in about a bizarre fracas in Gambell. I asked the Munz agent if I could hop on the plane when it got in from Gambell and head back there to arrest the two carpenters. He said he'd find a pilot for me; he felt the two incoming pilots were hurt too badly to fly again so soon.

I filled an airline bag with handcuffs, leg irons, belly chains, a billy club, and tear gas. I armed myself with three handguns, hoping the pilot could use one of them. Luckily he was a Vietnam vet, and he chose the .45 automatic.

We landed at Gambell. I had a plan. I jumped out of the plane, wearing jeans and a Pendleton shirt and looking like another construction man. I told the airport agent there that we had a load of building material and needed the carpenters to help unload it. Someone sought them out and told them to come to the plane to help unload. They were drunk, drinking beer out in the open in this normally dry village.

One of the carpenters came over to the open door of the plane. I poked a pistol in his face, handcuffed him, and placed him under arrest before he could think. I shoved him in the plane.

Then the other carpenter came over. He was a big guy, and I thought he would start something, but the same tactic worked. A .357 Colt poked between the eyes is a wonderful tonic for those disposed to rant and rave. Both men were now seated in the Commander, handcuffed and belly-chained and leg-ironed, strapped into their seats as I read them their rights, which was a new idea then.

The pilot slammed the door shut, and we were taxiing for takeoff before anyone on the ground was aware of what happened. I told the men that one move of any kind from either of them and I would shoot to kill, and I told them the pilot had the same orders. The pilot held up the .45 automatic and waved it at them.

"But I have to take a leak!" one man whined.

"Enjoy yourself," I told him.

I dumped the two men into the state jail in Nome without undue ceremony, and the district attorney was called. He was not happy to be the first DA in Alaska faced with a skyjacking, but it never came to that. There were so many charges that could be dumped on them for violation of FAA regulations that the FAA said to forget the FBI and skyjacking: these guys would be put away for quite a while anyway.

I was momentarily a hero with the flyboys for making the skies safe for air commerce, until Dick Gallagher at Munz Northern got a letter from the FAA charging his company with gross violations of FAA regulations for knowingly boarding intoxicated passengers and for allowing drinking in flight. So everyone got in trouble, the airline and the would-be skyjackers. Dick has never let me forget it. I stopped drinking at the Breakers Bar, too. ✈

Chapter 21

Funny Business  _____

Air sickness stories and other ghastly tales will never go out of style as long as there are rugged men in the northern air who like to display their bravado while looking down on everyone else as a weak-tummied lot.

Perhaps the oldest of the barf-bag stories comes from the group of transport pilots who worked the Kenai Peninsula for Pacific Northern Airways. Arnt Antonsen and his copilot often flew as passengers when other pilots were handling a plane. Sometimes they would be aboard when a new stewardess was making her first flight, and they would do their best to make the trip memorable.

With their airline jackets and caps out of sight, they would pretend to be regular passengers enjoying the flight. Then the one in the aisle seat would ask the new stewardess for an air sickness bag, claiming he was feeling queasy.

She would bring the folded-up white bag and hurry off to other duties, because the last thing she wanted was to have a sick passenger on her hands. The men would switch the empty bag for one that was already full of Dinty Moore beef stew as the fellow in supposed distress pretended to throw up.

This actor would then signal to the stewardess to take the open and brimful barf bag from his hands, adding a sickly smile to his pleading eyes. Just as she took hold of the bag, careful not to spill the contents, the fellow in the window seat would reach over, dip his fingers in, and come up with a big chunk of beef stew—which he would pop into his mouth.

"Hate to waste good chow," he would say to the shaken stewardess.

I saw the stunt pulled only once. It put the new employee in the john for the rest of the trip. She was ill and could not face another passenger.

MUD HOLE SMITH, president and driving force behind Cordova Air Lines, once competed many years ago for passengers on the run between Anchorage and Juneau by offering low fares and free champagne. The way Cordova flew the route, the flight was stretched out by stops for boarding folks at such fun places as Cordova, Yakutat, and Cape Yakataga near Icy Bay. For most passengers the leisurely flight in the big Constellation to the state capital was best taken in alcoholic stages anyway, sort of an in-flight training session before the real drinking began.

On one flight, the return stop at Cape Yakataga required the loading of a heavy section of bulldozer track. There wasn't enough room in the freight area, so the cargo master loaded the linked plates right into the passenger compartment, laying the tons of dirty steel down the center of the aisle.

Alaskans are used to such variety in their air travel. The passengers never lifted their eyebrows, and the Connie lurched into the sky, heading for its other stops and then on to Anchorage. But even with a full panel of instruments, the pilots couldn't cope with the intense fog that filled Cook Inlet and the Anchorage hinterlands. They circled over the area at an altitude that gave all the passengers a look at the solid blanket of wool below.

After an hour or so of this, even the most naive passengers began to suspect they might be running low on gas. But the stewardess anticipated their anxiety and took a stab at reassuring them.

"We may run out fuel," she announced brightly, appearing with an armload of bottles, "but we won't run out of champagne."

WIEN ALASKA AIRWAYS was one of the most reliable and well-loved airlines in the state. But even Wien could unnerve its passengers at times, as in this tale of fun and games on a flight from Nome to Fairbanks.

The crew was flying a Fairchild F-27, a fine twin-prop-jet, high-winged plane that was ideal for the rough fields and small passenger loads common to bush operations. On the flight up to Nome and Kotzebue, the pilot had trouble getting the right wing flap down. It refused to go down at the pilot's command—but then would lower itself without warning. The copilot was instructed to remedy the situation by using a wrench to manually work the flap down—doing this urgent duty via an access panel in the passenger cabin. The work did take a few minutes, with the copilot standing amid all the seated passengers.

On the way into Fairbanks, the copilot was stopped in his flap-lowering chore by a man who tapped him on the shoulder.

"What are you doing in there?" the curious passenger asked.

The copilot, not wanting to get involved in a lengthy technical explanation, said with a laugh, "Why, I am tightening the nut that holds the wing on; it was kind of loose."

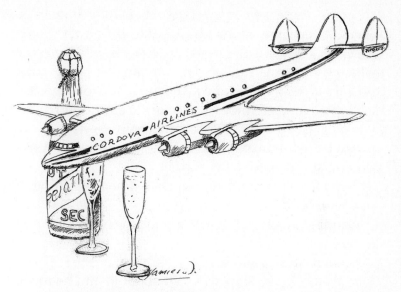

The passenger thought a minute and with his practical knowledge of mechanics yelled at the copilot, "But you're turning the wrench the wrong way; you're loosening it and the wing's gonna fall off!"

Now the other passengers were concerned. "Well, I think we got it tight enough to make Fairbanks," the copilot said as he quickly finished his job and scurried back to the privacy of the cockpit.

TWO WIEN F-27 DRIVERS were waiting for their passengers to board at Deadhorse, at the industrial airfield near Prudhoe Bay, on a winter day in 1970. When the mercury bottoms out in the minus 50s and less, everyone is bundled up in down parkas. Everyone from drillers to politicians looks pretty much the same, including airline pilots.

To amuse themselves while they waited, the pilots pretended to be drunk. As far as the other travelers were concerned, these were just a couple of rowdy fellow pass-engers. When it was about time to take off, one of the men yelled back toward the seated passengers, "Where the hell's those damned pilots; we're gonna be late getting into Fairbanks!" The loud conversation between the two men grew more and more critical of the airline and of the pilots who obviously were not on time.

After a few minutes, one of the make-believe drunks stood up and turned to his partner.

"Whaddya say we take a crack at flying this thing. It can't be so hard!"

And the two of them staggered into the cockpit, started the engines, and took off.

Their act didn't amuse everyone aboard. The supervi-sor at Wien's operations was told about it, and he made sure it was the pilots' last flight. ✈

Chapter 22

The Gamble

Once upon a time in Nome, six men were sitting around a kitchen table playing poker, and when not grumbling over their cards, sipping beer and whiskey. Higher and higher stakes wiped out three of them, and they stood and watched as the remaining three battled it out. When just about all the assets were in front of one man, the biggest loser shouted that he would put up his Aeronca airplane against the pile of cash and checks taking up most of the table. He wrote out a note on paper, using the aircraft ID number.

My shooting and hunting buddy Bob Workman was riding his luck that night. When the final card was turned over, he had a pile of money and an Aeronca airplane on skis. He had no pilot's license, but the players all agreed he had enough money to learn to fly the four-place plane— and some gas money besides.

In the dawn's early light, the group drove out to Municipal Field. The one-time owner pointed to a neat little red bird sitting pertly up on her skis. Snow covered the wings and fuselage, so the men jumped out and scraped it off.

There was some talk about taking a test hop and then

running up north across the Kougarok Mountains to take a few caribou.

When four of the men reported back to the little plane with their rifles and kit, there was barely room for them, heavily dressed as they were. With the whiskey still calling the moves, they squeezed into the plane and slid their guns on the floor beneath the seats. Luckily a high-pressure cell hung over the Seward Peninsula as the plane, without the blessing of a flight plan or a word to anyone, rose into the still, cold air and circled the field a few times.

After this brief familiarization with the controls, new pilot Bob Workman headed the plane northeast, happy as a lark that it flew so easily and smoothly.

The single-engine plane climbed into the clear air and offered the sleepy hunters a spectacular view of the Continental Divide that marches down the center of the peninsula. The droning of the engine and propeller had a mesmerizing effect on the occupants. With the warm air and smooth flight, not to mention the night of poker and drinking, they all fell asleep—including pilot Bob.

ONE OF THE PASSENGERS AWOKE and saw that the plane was in a shallow turn. He woke Bob. The sun was already past noon. The country below was totally alien to the men as they scanned the landscape. No one had any idea how long they had been flying.

Bob knew a great deal about the Seward Peninsula, where he had done a lot of hunting and fishing. But he had never seen the completely flat and featureless region below. They had no topo map to use in an attempt to relate to the geography below. Bob suggested they fly in a circle to see if they could find a village or a trapper's cabin.

Bob neglected to get a compass bearing on their route

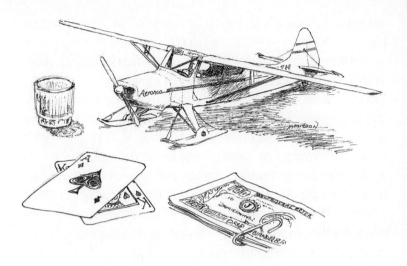

when he initiated a turn to the left. One of the men said the terrain below looked just like the frozen Arctic Ocean. They were truly lost. No one responded to their radio appeal for help.

The men didn't know it at the time, but they were flying above the smooth surface of frozen Selawik Lake, a thirty-one-mile-wide body of water that was more than a hundred miles northeast of where they originally planned to hunt. Some residents of Selawik village recall hearing a plane passing low, just out of sight. So do some of the folks at Noorvik, another village in the area. But the men didn't see the villages.

The men were afraid to fly away from the smooth area beneath them (which was the frozen lake) and were reluctant to strike out across the hills because they feared a disastrous landing when the gas ran out. They finally voted to land the plane on the smooth snow below them.

The original owner landed the plane on the snow and ended up running it at slow speed into a frozen object, perhaps the trunk of a tree that had washed into the lake. The men weren't hurt. They tried to stay warm by putting on all their clothing and by building a fire from materials in the plane. After a terrible night of shivering, Bob decided to walk out for help. Without map or compass, he had little idea where to direct his steps. He felt that if he walked long enough, he would run into a trapper or a villager or would be seen by someone flying by.

Finally a search effort got under way when people realized the four men were missing. Of course, no one knew where to look. At first, we simply searched in an ever-widening area from Nome. The search had gotten much more intense by the time we received a radio report from the Nome FAA that a survivor had been found walking near the edge of frozen Hotham Inlet, just above the Arctic Circle and a few miles south of Kotzebue.

The pilot who spotted the man found it odd that a lone walker was out on the ice of the inlet and that he seemed to be without pack or snowshoes. He buzzed the walker twice at low level but got no reaction. The man just kept walking. The pilot made another pass just above the snow, and the walking man again did not even notice the roaring plane.

The pilot landed on the snow behind the man. He had to run after him and pull him down to get him to stop walking. The man was Bob Workman.

Bob had walked for nearly thirty hours, traveling from a spot near the north-center of Selawik Lake to within a few miles of Kotzebue, without food and without stopping for rest. He walked some sixty miles.

Low-flying ski planes followed Bob's tracks back to the lake to find the other men. Bob's trek saved their lives.

Bob was transferred from one hospital to the next as

the experts worked on his frostbitten extremities. There was serious concern that he would lose both legs, but he refused to allow amputation. He was able to walk again after many weeks of physical therapy.

After his recovery, this level-headed guy who was always on top of things when we trekked in the mountains behind Nome said the near-tragic flight was "the funniest thing I ever did." He said he didn't know what got into him to undertake the flight. He said he should have known from previous experiments in flying in small aircraft that the engine and prop noise would put him to sleep.

Bob later decided to go back to school in Southern California for a degree in aeronautical engineering. Sad to say, he began experiencing severe pain in his legs while he was attending school, and the eventual diagnosis was cancer. He decided against having surgery, quit school, and returned to Nome, where he and his wife, Millie, had a few good weeks together before he died.

I think back to Bob's amazing flying adventure. A funny flight? Only in an ironic sense, and only the intrepid Bob Workman would describe it that way. ✈

Chapter 23

Winging It _____

Nome, being the aviation pioneering town that it is, loves a good show. When Bill Lear flew his Learjet up to Nome for a visit, we had a reindeer steak at the Bering Sea Hotel before he returned to Anchorage. I asked if he was going to make his usual takeoff. If so, I'd assemble a small crowd for the fun.

"Why not," he said.

With the immediate area clear of traffic and the FAA in on his typical routine for getting away fast, we watched Lear taxi to the extreme end of the runway and hold the brakes on the sleek jet until the tail was well off the ground and the engine was screaming. Then he let the brakes go and poured on the kerosene, crossing midfield at 180 to 200 miles per hour. Just before crossing the end-beacons, he turned the jet straight up for 10,000 feet before leveling out. It was quite a sight and had everyone cheering as he blasted up and almost out of sight.

I had been along on one of these takeoffs, and I knew that feeling when he turns straight up. Once up high, Lear would turn the jet over to its captain for the rest of the flight. Lear had no interest in flying flat.

I BRING IN LESTER BRONSON of Nome, state senator

and fine fellow, only because he is long gone and can't get at me anymore. Senator Bronson had a reputation as a flier. He was one of the first pilots I was warned to avoid, on land or air.

I got the word on the good senator one afternoon after I and my partner Gene Farland landed on a remote ocean beach near the mouth of the Sinuk River, just west of Nome. We had landed to investigate an overturned umiak half-buried in the sand. Gene was digging away at the bow of the skin-covered boat, looking for clues to the occupants, while I took photos of the scene.

Just then a single-engine plane came into view, saw us on the beach, and circled overhead.

"Oh, my God," Gene cried, "it's Bronson!"

I asked what the problem was as we watched Bronson's plane circle lower and lower. Farland grabbed a piece of driftwood and ran out to where the beach was clear of debris and wrote in big block letters in the sand: NO HELP NEEDED-TNX. The plane circled once more, then headed for Nome.

Gene explained that Bronson was infamous for piling up airplanes, even on a clear day with a beach a mile wide and twenty miles long. Unless we wanted to become involved in pulling the senator out of his crashed plane, we'd better be sure he lands somewhere else. Farland said it was hard to calculate how many planes Bronson had wrecked. He said most of the damage was done while attempting to help someone else—usually someone who didn't need help.

The reason Bronson was elected to office, I was told, was that he had crashed in most of the villages of the Seward Peninsula and got to know the voters there quite well—much better than anyone else running.

NO REPORT ON NORTHERN PILOTS would be complete without mention of Jules Thibidoux, who operated a flying service out of Barrow, at the "top of the world." Jules was well known for his forced landings in the arctic. They called him "Fly Out-Walk Back Thibidoux." He was a nice guy with a terrible piece of real estate to operate in, so he may have faced higher risks than most bush pilots.

Thibidoux invented a style of flying in the bush that was adopted by Howard Bowman and other pilots once they saw it used. It opened up a new avenue of dealing with short riverbanks and beaches and heavy loads.

When Howard first exposed me to the Thibidoux method of prelanding the airplane in the water without floats, I was certain that he had lost his mind—or that he was trying to impress me with a sharp landing and had simply failed.

Thibidoux had taken a contract from an oil exploration party to deliver diesel fuel to a campsite on Maybe Creek near the Colville River. He was able to deliver the fuel with his rickety Stinson Voyager 108, beating out operators with Super Cubs and the like, by concocting the technique of landing his wheel plane several yards short of the shoreline and rolling up on the hardpan from the water on momentum and with some gunning. Taking off was easy without the load of fuel.

This sandbar-hopping became a staple of Howard Bowman's, and he proved a master of it over the years. In one memorable case, Bowman made several "splash landings" on a Colville River site, delivering men and equipment to help in the rescue of a downed Super Cub. Watching his plane approach was scary, as the big tundra tires presented such a blunt obstacle to the placid water. But the braking action of the water, a true hydraulic brake,

always slowed the plane and allowed a roll-up on the shore with the load.

IT WAS THE COMMON PRACTICE at Kotzebue during winter to pull up to the main street in your ski plane and let the engine idle while you took on a cup of coffee and a stale doughnut. The planes were seldom tied up or anchored in any way. The planes were up against an icy embankment, and the pilots were near enough to run out and shut the engine off if a plane started to creep along on its skis.

Nonchalance was born at that place as the really cool polar-bear pilots like Leon Shellabarger would sit down to a hearty breakfast with their backs to the shop window, never giving their idling aircraft a glance until they paid the cashier and came out. This despite the fact that some planes had a reputation for creepy throttles that would advance the idle, causing the plane to jerk forward.

If a plane's engines were left off for long, the oil would return to a tarlike consistency and the engine would not start at all without firepotting. This involved applying high heat from a Coleman stove to the underside of a blanketed engine. Firepotting required avid attention. If the blanket caught fire, you could usually save the day by just yanking it off the cowl and beating it out. But every so often the engine itself, loaded with gasoline and oil, would catch fire, requiring a quick shot with a bottle of carbon dioxide. Pilots who left their firepotted plane and got too involved with their waffles and syrup often found their beloved Cessna or Piper halfway burned to the frame before they knew what was happening.

There were wags who would watch as a pilot dashed in for coffee and a cruller after firepotting his plane and would move the firepot rig over to a look-alike plane. Most Super Cubs shared a common outline. When the pilot came out to check, he would discover that he had apparently firepotted the wrong plane! Other practical jokers liked to slip a cube of Limburger cheese into the map pocket of a friend's plane on a fine summer day. There are a lot of ways to drive a pilot nuts.

PILOT RUTH HURST had a favorite bush pilot story. The tale sounds odd, but it's so likely to have happened that I'm sure it really did.

A young fellow was trying to get started flying a Super Cub out to the villages around Unalakleet. He would offer rides into the big city of Unalakleet (population about 300). He took off one day, with just a few snowflakes fluttering down, and headed for Shaktoolik, up the coast on Norton Sound. The weather worsened, and he found himself flying lower and lower, trying to maintain visual contact with the icy edge of the sea. Soon he was blasting his way through whiteout and heavy flurries of thick flakes. There was no good place to land and sit out the storm, so he hung onto the coastal ice rim, hoping to find a flat place where he could bring the Cub down.

He continued with nothing but canned-milk visibility. He felt the Cub hit a bump—what he assumed was a spot of rough air. The prop kept churning up so much snow that he could just see the spinner and a few feet on either side.

Suddenly there was a pounding on the side of the Cub. He looked. An Eskimo was standing there in a deep snowdrift, knocking on the side of the plane.

The Eskimo told the pilot that he had heard the plane come down into the drift behind his cabin at the reindeer camp, and he wondered why the pilot didn't shut the engine off and come in for some coffee. The pilot stepped out to see his little plane all but buried in the snowdrift. The prop had been churning up a flurry, but the Cub was going nowhere. ✈

Chapter 24

Wild Life _____

One of the oddest bits of aviation misfortune I've ever run across befell Doc Cunningham of Palmer, a fine pilot and an FAA medical examiner. This was back some years ago when it was legal to fly into an area and hunt the same day, allowing hunters to get their big bull moose for the freezer in just a single day's work.

When Doc and his son landed at the strip where they were going to begin their moose walk, they saw a pilot walking around his plane, dropping a stream of something from a large box.

"Whatcha doin', ol' buddy?" Doc asked.

The pilot said he was surrounding his plane with a trail of mothball crystals to keep the porcupines away. Porcupines wouldn't cross such a barrier, he said, and at this strip they were in the habit of chewing on aircraft tires.

Doc and his son laughed when they heard this old wives' tale and proceeded to go hunting. They saw the other pilot take off three hours later. When they returned to the plane after a successful hunt, packing sections of their bull, they found the tail wheel chewed off. They had to jack up the rear of the Cessna and use all their friction tape to reform the remains of the tire so they could take

off and then land again at home without ground-looping or worse.

Back at Palmer, Doc suddenly realized he had parked his fine Weatherby rifle near the plane but had neglected to pack it for the trip home. He raced back to the tiny airstrip.

From the air, Doc could see that the rifle was still there. He felt relieved until he landed and taxied over to it. The fine stock was eaten right down to the through bolt and some other metal parts by porcupines—a two-hundred-dollar loss.

HARRY YOST, a Marine buddy of mine from Korea, moved to Alaska after completing a mini-career in the

Oregon State Police. He wanted to find out what there was to do in life besides chasing speeders on Interstate 5. Harry earned money for flying lessons by building chicken crates for Alaska Airlines, which flew thousands of chickens from Seattle up to Palmer, Alaska, every spring for the drumstick and egg farmers there.

As he got into the work, Harry learned some surprising things about his new trade. For instance, the ammonia given off by the droppings of a chicken can be pretty strong stuff. Multiply it by three thousand chickens in a cargo plane, and you're in deep shit. The aroma could thicken the common air shared by birds and crew until the men were crying at the controls.

Another complicating factor in these fowl airlifts was that the birds couldn't be flown above 8,000 feet if they were to stay healthy. The air was too thin. So it was low and slow flying all the way from Seattle to Palmer.

Then Alaska Airlines got smart and decided to use pressurized cargo planes. They would load their fast, sleek Constellations with Harry Yost's crates, full of the tasty birds, and zip them to Palmer at high altitude, keeping the inside air pressure at less than 8,000 feet.

The plan was fine with the chickens, but the air conditioning system went redline when it quickly overloaded with ammonia fumes from the fryers who failed to use the regular john. As mechanics tried to repair the overloaded air system while the plane sat at the airport in Seattle, the cargo of six thousand birds quietly died. Harry still refuses to eat any kind of chicken while aboard Alaska Airlines.

A FRIEND OF MINE INSISTED I tell the story of Bob Burkholder of the U.S. Fish and Wildlife Service, who turned a simple flight into a memorably funny tale. Burkholder was asked to ferry a Super Cub from McGrath to Anchorage. He took off from the gravel field at McGrath for the 250-mile trip back home, but after a few minutes aloft, he decided he needed to answer a call of nature. He found a lake that suited his needs and made a nice float landing.

When he was ready to leave, he applied throttle to the idling engine and attempted to lift off. He wasn't paying attention, and to his surprise, he ran out of water for the takeoff, and he crashed the plane at the water's edge.

This wasn't Burkholder's first crash. He was just lucky that all of his crashes were the kind one could walk or swim away from. On this occasion, another Fish and Wildlife Service plane soon landed and picked him up.

The accident had to be reported, so Burkholder got on the radio in the rescue plane and called Rosie, the base office factotum. She had the onerous duty of taking the crash details from Burkholder and relaying them by another radio system to Fish and Wildlife headquarters in Juneau.

Burkholder tried to minimize damage to the Super Cub as he radioed in his report while the other pilot circled the crash scene. The boss in Juneau wanted to know how badly the plane was damaged, so he sent questions over the air through Rosie to Burkholder.

"Yeah, the wings look OK," Burkholder said in answer to one question. "No serious damage there."

"The tail isn't damaged at all, Chief! Perfectly OK."

"The prop is probably OK; it looks OK from here."

The next question relayed by Rosie was about the windshield.

"The windshield?" he replied.

Well, he couldn't see the windshield. He decided to tell the whole truth. In a whisper, he confessed over the radio:

"Rosie, the damn thing sunk!"

BOB TARNOWSKI gets the last word in this chapter of Alaska aerial oddities. Tarnowski, who was a veteran bush pilot and in the old days an aerial wolf hunter, had just landed his Cub at the Fairbanks strip when another veteran bush pilot, Sandy Jamieson, came along and noticed that the aircraft had more resemblance to a porcupine than to anything that flies. Branches stuck through the fabric on every surface and much of the covering was gone from the wings.

Jamieson walked up to the old pilot and asked what happened.

"Well, you see, I hit a bird," Tarnowski told him.

"What kind of bird did you hit?" Jamieson asked.

"Well, I never did find out what kind of bird it was," Tarnowski confessed, "because when I hit it, it was on its nest and the nest was in a tree." ✈

Chapter 25

High Jinx

Pushing the limits on load capacity is a favorite bush-pilot game. Take Archie Ferguson, whose old plane was overdue in Kotzebue on the northwest Alaska coast after a flight to Candle, where he had some diggings. Pilots coming in to Kotzebue were asked to make a preliminary search en route for any downed aircraft. A few minutes later, the pilot of an inbound Stinson on skis reported a plane on the snow, on the skinny part of the Baldwin Peninsula. The pilot circled the downed plane, and as he watched from 500 feet, he saw a growing number of people emerge from the craft.

He landed to offer his help and found Archie Ferguson, who was trying to fly a bunch of village kids and their mothers in from Candle. The pilot of the Stinson had room for five of the kids, and he flew them on to Kotzebue. On the way, one kid told him that Archie's plane never really got up into the air at all, but kept bouncing along the snow and ice. The passengers thought that was a lot of fun. Counting babies and himself, Archie had twelve people aboard his four-place airplane.

ARCHIE'S NEPHEW, DON, and I went fishing one Fourth of July up on the confluence of the Kelly and

Noatak rivers, well north of the Arctic Circle, where there were no game limits. We could catch all the fish we wanted.

We kept fishing until we had two large gunny sacks full of Dolly Varden and rainbow trout. Don insisted his Super Cub could lift the huge sacks plus both of us when it came time to go home. We were there until after midnight, shooting some fishing action pictures under the midnight sun. Then we tried to take off. The tail of the plane refused to lift off the sandbar. We had to leave all but twenty of these great trout on the sandbar so we could get airborne. Don planned to return for the rest of the trout later that morning. We wanted them badly for smoking.

Don Ferguson dropped me off in Kotzebue and flew back for the trout. But all he found was shredded gunny sacks and the size-twenty-two footprints of a hungry bear.

ARCHIE FERGUSON HAD ANOTHER ADVENTURE the day he flew a load of freight from Nome to the Native village of Elim, east of Nome on Norton Sound. Archie was afraid the Elim airstrip might be muddy because the winter snow and ice were breaking up but the long, dry summer days hadn't yet arrived. He ran into an Eskimo from Elim who was working in Nome and asked how the airstrip was.

"Pilot land there last week," the villager told him.

Archie loaded his Cessna bush plane and took off for Elim, not a very long flight. The weather was great, and he could see the field clearly. It looked a bit soggy to him, so he went around and looked it over again at a lower elevation. For some reason, he decided it was OK to land. He said to himself that if the other pilot landed there, he

certainly could.

The wheels of his plane dug furrows in the mud before they quickly stopped rolling, and the Cessna turned over on its back. Archie was not happy. After unloading the plane and repairing the damage, he flew back to Nome and sought out the man from Elim who had given him the bum advice.

"I landed there and my plane turned over on its back!" Archie complained to the villager.

The Eskimo replied, "Other pilot do same thing."

I'VE OFTEN THOUGHT how funny a video would be that captured some of my crazy moments in the air. On one trip from Nome to St. Michael, with Ray Decker the pilot, we flew in circles more than we flew straight. There was a terrible whiteout. We were both crazy to even consider going, but Ray needed the money and I had to get to St. Mike to check out some police problem.

A diagram of our flight as far as Moses Point would look like a drawing of a loose coil spring—dozens of connected circles at various altitudes as we tried to figure out where the hell we were. We were all-too-near the shoreline of Norton Sound, and our forward motion was all dependent upon one of us spotting some dark object, such as a shrub, which Ray could use as a visual anchor while we sprang forward to find another clue on the landscape. I don't think we ever flew above a hundred feet—and mostly much less. Our cabin conversation sounded like a comedy routine.

"Hey, Ray, there's a big bush next to a black rock. Got it?"

"That ain't much. Get something out farther—like that!" And he'd pull the plane forward a few hundred more feet.

"I got a log shack near the shore ice on the far right!"

"I don't remember such a shack, but let's see." And he would circle over it until we caught a half-mile opening along the shore ice where it looked like we could break into the clear. Off he would go, more than likely to be faced again with the same canned-milk visibility.

I recall his plaintive cry when we seemed to be doomed to circle a rather large shrub forever because we couldn't find any other landmarks. "Hang onto that bush while I look around!" he shouted. And my eyes would not leave the bush as he circled around, looking for the next object to tie us visually to the ground.

We broke out into clear air around Shaktoolik, where we skirted over the reindeer pens and the herder's shack. The next thing we found was a flat island to our right and the lights of Unalakleet runway stretching out to meet us as Ray brought the Gull Wing in.

"We better get more gas here," Ray said. "We burned a lot over Rocky Point." As soon as the plane rolled to a stop, Ray was out of the plane and onto the ground, taking a pee. "Sure makes you want to go, all that bush flying," he said with a laugh. I helped him irrigate the runway as I thought about how good it was going to be to get a piece of pie at the Unalakleet restaurant, where Theckla would have it warming over the range.

AFTER SETTLING A POLICE CASE in St. Michael, I was ready to return to Nome. Pilot Ray Decker spent his time at the trading post or store while I concluded my affairs. Ray felt it was smart for a pilot so close to the country here to keep out of the business of the law. I'm not saying that Ray wouldn't step in and help if I had trouble with some prisoner, but otherwise he was Mr. Discreet, knowing that next week or next month, the same fellow I had in irons might be a paying customer with a wife and three kids.

I was in charge of getting a crowd of people onto the plane for the flight out. It was a darkening afternoon. Everyone had to get out, and there was no time for a return trip. I had a violent prisoner in leg irons and belly chain. I also had a very sick and perhaps insane woman, doped up with sleeping pills and wrapped in an Army surplus mummy bag. The local magistrate, Mary Bahr, a lady in her late sixties or early seventies, needed a ride home to Unalakleet. And we also had to take an orphaned child, who was hungry and tired and scared to death.

Ray saw the crowd gathering to board his four-place Stinson Gull Wing and told me, no way. I managed to talk him into taking us all. Before boarding, we had to free the plane from a hole that had trapped one wheel. With help from villagers and a long plank, we got the plane onto a stretch of solid but humpy ground, not quite frozen yet for the winter. There were some shrubs and trees to the right, and downhill from us was the village cemetery, with its picket fence offering little privacy or security for the souls resting there.

Ray then loaded the passengers. The chained prisoner

was put on the floor under my seat, with his feet to the rear. The mummified woman went in the middle on the floor, with her face and head in front of the rear bench. Mary Bahr sat in the middle rear, with the kid on one side and my typewriter and camera case on the other. I sat in the right-hand seat, my boots on the prisoner's shoulders.

St. Mike had no runway. We had one shot to get the big bird into the air, or there would be splinters and bodies strewn across the snow-covered cemetery. Ray revved the radial engine until it shook the whole plane as he held the brakes on. He had us all lean as far forward as we could in order to improve the balance point. The Gull Wing shuddered and shook as Ray edged the power up. All of a sudden he yelled "Here we go! Pray!"

The plane rolled a few feet and hit a soft spot, skewing it a bit. It rolled faster and then began bouncing as the propeller demanded that the plane fly. There was another bounce and then a crashing sound as the plane plowed through the cemetery fence, then leaped into the air—free.

Ahead, we could see the black waters and chunk ice of Norton Sound and then the twinkling lights of Unalakleet. We made it to Unalakleet, where we dropped Mary Bahr off, and then raced into Nome to beat the worst of a weather front that was moving across Norton Sound. It was the end of another act of high comedy in Alaska's ongoing sky follies. ✈

About the Author_____

Joe Rychetnik sits atop a peak overlooking the Ruth Glacier in 1970.

Joe Rychetnik is a veteran of the World War II invasion of Okinawa and was a U.S. Marines photographer during the Korean War. He began collecting his Alaska aviation tales after coming to the new state in 1959 as Anchorage bureau chief for *United Press International.* Following a stint with the *Anchorage Daily Times,* he switched from reporter to cop, working as state trooper in a far-flung district that included Nome, Kotzebue, and Barrow.

Back at the *Times* in 1964, Rychetnik captured scenes of the devastating Good Friday earthquake in a series of memorable photos. His next career move turned into seven years as Alaska correspondent for *Time-Life News Service.*

Rychetnik later went into public relations work in California. He is the author of *Bush Cop,* about the Alaska State Troopers. He and his wife, Glenda, now live in Palm Springs, California. ✈

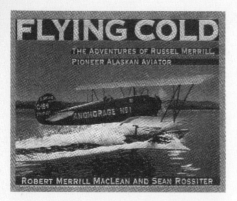

FLYING COLD

The Adventures of Russell Merrill, Pioneer Alaska Bush Pilot

by Robert Merrill MacLean and Sean Rossiter

Trained as a pilot during W.W.I, Russel Merrill was determined to spend his life flying. His love of flight lured him from Oregon to Alaska, the frontier of aviation, where Merrill piloted the first airplanes to fly into Petersburg, Wrangell, Kodiak, and Anchorage.

In Alaska, where travel across the wilderness was measured in days or weeks, he challenged dangerous terrain, severe climates, and mechanical failures to bring aviation to remote communities. Merrill forever changed the scope of northern history and commerce as a prominent member of the territory's first graduating class of bush pilots who earned their wings in the school of hard-earned experience.

Retail price: hardbound ($34.95) and paperback ($24.95)
Size: 192 pages, 10" by 9", 75 B&W photos.
ISBN: 0-945397-32-1 (HB), 0-945397-33-X (PB)

To find a copy of FLYING COLD, visit your local bookstore. Or, send a check for the purchase price (plus 8.2% sales tax on orders from Washington state) and $3 for postage and handling to: Epicenter Press, Box 82368, Kenmore, WA 98028. Visa/MC orders may be phoned to 206-485-6822, or faxed to 206-481-8253.